Soon this brief pilgrimage will be over,
and we shall be for ever with the Lord.
We shall see Him as He is: what a hope!
May the Lord bless and encourage you, Jim.

Martin

LIFE

BEYOND THE SUNSET

Glimpses of Heaven in Scripture

MARTIN GIRARD

Cover Pictures:

Sunset beyond Les Hanois Lighthouse, Guernsey, Channel Islands: 30 April, 2013.

Scripture taken from the King James Version of the Bible.

First Printing: 2017

ISBN: 978-1-326-98252-2

SKY-WAY MESSAGES
40, The Mead
Liphook, Hants, GU30 7AT. U.K.

www.skywaymessages.co.uk

Dedication:

To the glory of God and to the memory of those dear saints of His who, like Abraham, desired "a better country" (Hebrews 11:16) and who encouraged me to be interested in the eternal home of Christ's redeemed people. May it inspire our three children and their generation to "seek those things which are above" (Colossians 3:1) too.

Contents

Acknowledgements

When a list of acknowledgements is compiled by a believer, it must surely begin with the Lord. As Scripture reminds us, "Except the LORD build the house, they labour in vain that build it" (Psalm 127:1). Without His help nothing of any lasting value can be achieved. In my initial preparation I sought His direction, and I can only thank Him for the way in which He guided my thinking and enabled an outline to be developed.

A very pertinent prayer of dependence is found in Psalm 119: "Open thou mine eyes, that I may behold wondrous things out of thy law" (v.18). What wonderful treasures are there! All we need are *opened eyes* to *behold* them – and it is the Spirit of God who must reveal those truths to us. Without God's Word we would know nothing about heaven. The messages I have given find their origin in Scripture, and the studies are all centred in the Word. The author therefore acknowledges "help from above" in preparing and preaching those messages, and in putting them into print. The Lord Jesus said, "Without me ye can do nothing" (John 15:5). Accordingly, thanks must rightly be rendered to **Him** – and if you are blessed by what you read in the following chapters, please direct *your* thanks to Him too.

Many resources are available to assist us nowadays. Over the years material written by others has been read and will have made an impression upon my mind, perhaps almost subconsciously. Strong's Exhaustive Concordance of the Bible has been an invaluable tool in my studies. Then there is the computer! In this sophisticated age it is no longer necessary to write everything out laboriously by hand. Word-processing at the computer has made things so much easier!

In my earlier Dedication I referred to those saints of God who inspired me in years past. Without being unnecessarily repetitive, I confess that I owe a great debt to a number of dear believers who had an influence upon my life during formative years – and later. Sometimes we only appreciate what we owe to others when they have gone from us. It is good to thank God for those who knew what it was *to seek first the kingdom of God, and his righteousness* (Matthew 6:33). We remember such with gratitude.

One person who must be singled out, however, is Jim North from Landford Wood Mission Hall. Knowing that he had experience in publishing, I asked him about a possible Foreword for this book. As a qualified English teacher, I believed editing would be unnecessary – but Jim had other ideas! His astute mind was soon busily employed in revealing inconsistencies in the text and suggesting alternatives. Initially the proverbial red pen was perceived to be an intrusion, but by the time Jim's painstaking work was completed I had come to see it as a necessary part of the publishing procedure. Even teachers are not immune from further teaching! Jim's diligence and patience throughout have been greatly appreciated. My wife is a Yorkshire lass, and I have come to appreciate the blunt and forthright way in which Yorkshire folk are known to express themselves. Knowing that Jim was from Sheffield, I mentioned to him early on that I could "call a spade a spade" in communicating with him. The reply I received was unique: "Being a Yorkshire man I do not call a spade "a spade"; I call it *a shovel!*"

Although the text has been subjected to ruthless editing, errors may have slipped through the net. They always do! Please let me know if you discover any, for we have "not … already attained" and are not "already perfect" (Philippians 3:12); but one day "we shall all be changed" (1 Corinthians 15:51). Praise God!

Martin Girard

May 2017

Introduction

Life Beyond the Sunset

The evening Bible study was over, and before returning to our homes a short time was spent conversing with one another. One friend chatted to me and raised a subject which was to be significant. He described how, some years before, he had been travelling on a cross-Channel ferry. It was a beautiful evening, clear and calm, and passengers were enjoying being on the deck of the ship. The sun was setting, and a lorry driver standing near my friend was watching the spectacle. As the crimson ball of fire disappeared beneath the distant horizon, the driver turned to my friend and exclaimed, "Nature's wonderful." It had been a perfect sunset, and it had made a real impression on all who had seen it. My friend knew that the beauty of that sunset was more than a manifestation of one of the wonders of nature. It was a proclamation of "the glory of God" (Ps.19:1) that had been witnessed.

A perfect sunset can almost be a medicine to the soul. It speaks powerfully to our innermost being, making us aware of our own mortality and of that "otherness" beyond and above us. Often I have stood quietly along Guernsey's pretty coastline in the Channel Islands and have watched that vast flaming orb sink beneath "the rosy-tinted west" — as Fanny Crosby called it in her hymn *Some day the silver cord will break*. Guernsey's west coast is a photographer's paradise on an almost-cloudless evening. Many are there with cameras poised to record the sun sinking beyond the horizon. My own spirit has been touched as I have watched the sun disappear from view. It is a sight not to be missed.

Often we say that one thing leads to another, and this is certainly the case with this book. A year or so previously I had written and published *Living in Life's Evening*, a book of sermons based on the lives of "senior citizens" in the Bible. As that book reached its publication, I began to think about a sequel. *Living in Life's Evening* dealt with the *end* of life – but what lies *beyond*? Sunset may indicate the close of "life's little day" (as Henry Francis Lyte called it) but what about *after* the sunset? When the sun has set upon our earthly life, what will life be like for the believer in eternity?

Hymns about heaven have, generally, gone out of fashion. Look at the hymn books of a previous generation and see how many hymns on the theme of heaven can be found in Sankey's *Sacred Songs & Solos* or in *Golden Bells*. The reason that so many of these lovely hymns have disappeared and cannot be found in modern song books is not simply one of fashion. I firmly believe that the Christian's heavenly hope has been lost sight of and many professing believers have become comfortable in this world. When that happens, "aspirations after heaven" (as Sankey called a section in his hymn book) become superfluous. Should any disagree with my premise, I am quick to point out that we must never derive our theology from hymn books, however good those hymn books may be. The fact remains, however, that godly and gifted poets in the past composed some beautiful pieces that are true to Scripture, and these help to direct our minds and hearts to our eternal home.

While these thoughts were echoing in my mind, an elderly Christian lady joined us for lunch one Sunday. It was the 27th September, 2014 — less than nine months before the Lord called her home. During her time with us she raised the subject of what life will be like when we get to heaven. The thoughts that she expressed made me smile inwardly, because during the preceding week I had begun to research that very subject! Her comments, and those of my friend who described the sunset he remembered, were being used by the Lord to propel me towards a series of messages from Scripture on the subject of heaven. *Life Beyond the Sunset* was the title that at once sprang to mind, for it seemed to follow on quite naturally from *Living in Life's Evening*. I also felt inspired by Virgil Brock's moving hymn *Beyond the Sunset* which is quoted in full later.

Hymns can have a profound effect upon us, and this is why we ought to gravitate towards those that glorify God and are true to Scripture. In my studies of *life beyond the sunset* I have linked in ten hymns with the messages. Some of these hymns are better known than others. The following pages are very much a transcript of ten sermons delivered on this theme.

This is the sort of book that an author will never feel satisfied with — for the simple reason that we know so little about heaven. This side of eternity it will always be an incomplete book. In the following pages I have attempted to view "the land that is very far off" (Isa.33:17). If the contents of this book make us long for heaven and learn to regulate our lives *now* in preparation for our entrance to the celestial city, it will have been worth writing it.

Beyond the Sunset

Beyond the sunset, O blissful morning,
When with our Saviour heav'n is begun.
Earth's toiling ended, O glorious dawning;
Beyond the sunset, when day is done.

Beyond the sunset no clouds will gather,
No storms will threaten, no fears annoy;
O day of gladness, O day unending,
Beyond the sunset, eternal joy!

Beyond the sunset a hand will guide me
To God, the Father, whom I adore;
His glorious presence, His words of welcome,
Will be my portion on that fair shore.

Beyond the sunset, O glad reunion,
With our dear loved ones who've gone before;
In that fair homeland we'll know no parting,
Beyond the sunset for evermore!

Virgil P. Brock

Chapter 1

The Old Testament Canvas

When the mists have rolled in splendour
From the beauty of the hills,
And the sunlight falls in gladness
On the rivers and the rills,
We recall our Father's promise
In the rainbow of the spray:
We shall know each other better
When the mists have rolled away.

We shall know, as we are known,
Nevermore to walk alone,
In the dawning of the morning
Of that bright and happy day,
We shall know each other better,
When the mists have rolled away!

Annie H. Barker

One of the most magnificent scenes anyone can imagine is that of a clear sky and the sun setting over the ocean. There is something overwhelming about a scene like that. A sunset over the land is certainly beautiful, with rays of light emanating across the darkening landscape from the setting sun. But nothing compares with the sun setting over the open sea. There is something almost poetic about such a scene. How many of us, I wonder, have stood on an unclouded evening and have watched the setting sun gradually slip from sight until its last fragment disappeared beyond the distant horizon? Photographers, whether professional or amateur, love such a spectacle. They can often be seen endeavouring to capture each moment of the silent drama as it unfolds. That sparkling highway of

1

light across the rippling waves, leading onwards to the setting sun, is stirring and mystical. It seems to be a passage to another world, and we feel drawn magnetically to step out on a journey that will take us beyond the confines of time.

As we watch the sun setting in silent majesty over the ocean, profound thoughts can arise within the mind — thoughts about life and its purpose, and questions about the afterlife. The boundless ocean surely speaks to us of life itself. It is only a sunset as far as *we* are concerned. Out beyond the horizon to the west lies another shore where the light is still bright and clear. While *we* are enjoying a tranquil evening before the twinkling stars appear and display their own ethereal glory, *others* are experiencing the ever-increasing brightness of a new day.

A nagging question often arises within the mind as we watch the sun going down. If light continues in other parts of the world out to the west of us, and life goes on under the undimmed brightness of the sun, could something similar happen in the *spiritual* realm? Just as one day follows another in the natural world, could it be that another life exists *beyond* the one to which we are tethered? *Is there life "beyond the sunset"?* Like that pathway of light from the setting sun, is there a highway leading us into another world?

This is a theme that I want to explore in this book by turning to the pages of Holy Scripture. God, our Heavenly Father, has not left us to grope in the darkness of a hopeless night. In His Word He has made known to us that other world beyond our own — the life that goes on beyond the sunset. Heaven is *His* abode.

The very first verse of the Bible informs us that in the beginning "God created the heaven and the earth" (Gen.1:1). He purposed that "a firmament" should exist over us, to separate the waters above from the waters beneath (Gen.1:6). The Hebrew word *raqia,* which is translated as "firmament", means *an expanse*. It signifies something thinly spread out. Biblical scholars have identified three "heavens" in Scripture: the atmospheric heaven, the stellar heaven, and "heaven" where God's throne is located. The word "firmament" (used elsewhere in Scripture) can apply to any of these concepts, but in Genesis 1 it appears to refer to the atmosphere above us.

Man, divinely created in God's image, was made to inhabit the earth and was placed in the perfect environment of Eden. It would appear that God intended man to live for ever. One prohibition only existed in Eden. The "tree of the knowledge of good and evil" was the one tree that was to be left alone. All other trees could be enjoyed and their fruit eaten, but if the fruit of this particular tree was taken and consumed it would result in death (Gen.2:17). The implication is that if man had left that tree alone he would not have died. Of course, we know the consequences. Man disobeyed his Creator and brought sin, death, and ruin into our world. (See Romans 5:12.)

Another Scene

I would like you to imagine a different scene. It is one that I do not find difficult to picture in my own mind as I have seen it on a number of occasions. About five miles from our home in the south of England, there is a viewpoint. A winding country road climbs a hillside and turns a corner. As it does so, a beautiful view opens up to the right. Through a wooden gate, and above the level of a bramble-filled hedge, can be seen the rolling hills of West Sussex. In the foreground is the Rother Valley, and beyond it can be seen the South Downs. Sometimes that view can be completely obscured. Under the correct conditions, a morning mist can form in the valley, making it appear momentarily that you are looking across the sea to a headland on the far side. The distant hills are still visible, but the valley itself is filled with mist. Everything in that valley is hidden from sight.

Those of us who live in the area know what can happen next. As the

3

temperature rises and the sun breaks through, the mist will gradually be burned away. When that happens, all that lay hidden behind the mist is revealed.

That scene illustrates the spiritual atmosphere of the Old Testament. We discover, in Scripture, that in Old Testament times people were very much in a mist and could see only a little of the future. For instance, consider a verse in the Psalms. "For this God is our God for ever and ever: he will be our guide even unto death." (Ps.48:14). Initially, this is a comforting verse. It is certainly wonderful to know that God can be *our* God for ever and that He will guide us through life, but there is something unknown too. "He will be our guide *even unto death*" [emphasis added] — but what about *after* death? Will we not need that guidance after death? What can we *expect* after death? Verses like this do not furnish a complete answer.

However, at the same time there is an unwavering hope running all through the Old Testament. The promised Messiah, introduced in Genesis 3, never vanishes from the sacred text. Zechariah describes Him arriving in triumph on the Mount of Olives (Zech.14:4) and tells us that "the LORD shall be king over all the earth: in that day shall there be one LORD, and his name one" (Zech.14:9). Obviously that "day" is not literally one of twenty-four hours. It is an unending period of time in which great blessing will be experienced.

The opening verses of Ecclesiastes 3 tell us plainly that there is a time for every activity under heaven. But the passage goes on to state that God has placed eternity in the heart of man (Eccl.3:11). Literally, the Hebrew expression used means "the age" and is translated as "eternity" in most modern versions of the Bible. (The Authorised Version renders it "the world".) We have been created with the capacity to look beyond the events of time because God has placed the concept of *eternity* in our hearts. Of course, that does not mean that we understand it! God's thoughts are as far above ours as the heavens are above the earth (Isa.55:9). The human mind can never fathom what it means for something to be unending. Yet we do have awareness of eternity and of "something beyond" within our hearts. This is why the psalmist can envisage giving thanks unto God "for ever" (Ps.30:12).

In this chapter so far, we have been thinking of pictures. In order to embark upon a study of the life that continues after death, we must start at the beginning and consider what we are told in the Old Testament. We are therefore going to paint a very broad picture of how life after death was viewed in that bygone era. It is necessary to use a very thick brush upon the Old Testament canvas for the undeniable reason that fine details are simply not there. The picture we are creating is very much one of a valley filled with mist.

Three broad lines are to be developed in this chapter — and I stress that they are all *broad*. We shall consider truth's *dawning* and its *development*, before examining its *destination* and seeing where it leads us.

Truth's Dawning

We must begin our study by looking at *the Patriarchs' faith* in Hebrews 11. The whole chapter is about faith and begins with Abel. He knew the importance of approaching God by means of sacrifice rather than on the ground of his own efforts, and he was declared righteous because he drew near to his Creator in the divinely-appointed way. Enoch also demonstrated faith, and because his life brought pleasure to God he was taken from this earth without having to face death. Noah, too, was a man whose faith caused him to obey God. As a result, he built the ark and escaped the divine judgment of the Flood.

Although each of these characters displayed faith, it is Abraham who is the first person to demonstrate faith of the kind that we are considering here. The summary of his life in Hebrews 11 tells us that Abraham responded to the call of God and set out on a journey, not knowing where that journey would take him. Like Enoch who earlier had walked with God and was then miraculously transported to heaven, Abraham displayed the *pilgrim* spirit. A place that he would receive "for an inheritance" had been promised, and Abraham journeyed steadfastly towards his goal. He built no home out of bricks or stone but was a tent-dweller throughout his life, because he was looking for a city with foundations, "whose builder and maker is God" (Heb.11:8—10). What did Abraham have in mind? Which city on this earth has been built by God?

Abraham "died in faith, not having received the promises, but having seen them afar off" (Heb.11:13). He was "persuaded" of the promises. He had no doubt in his mind that God said what He meant and meant what He said, and Abraham "embraced" those promises. It was as though he took those promises in both arms and pressed them to his heart. How could he doubt the One who had called him? His confession that he was a stranger and a pilgrim was backed up by his life. He was a man going somewhere; but where was he going? The next verses explain that he was seeking "a country" — one that was very different from the country of his origin. Had he been mindful of that country, he had every opportunity to return. But his eye was set upon "a better country", one that was "heavenly", and God had prepared a city for him (Heb.11:14—16). Here we have the truth declared clearly and plainly: Abraham was the first person to be seeking "a city" (v.10) and "a country" (v.14) that were *heavenly* in origin. This is the dawning of the truth that we are considering.

Having been made aware of Abraham's *faith*, we must turn our attention to his *future*. It is important to remember that this future was *heavenly* (v.16). Both the city and the country that Abraham sought were outside of this world. Someone reading these pages might, quite rightly, question our approach. This chapter set out to

6

explore *life beyond the sunset* from an Old Testament perspective, but we have been using Hebrews 11 which is very much a New Testament passage! To develop the subject along Old Testament lines we need to go back to Genesis 23 and to the death of Sarah. Abraham's beloved wife had died, and he wanted to give her a respectful burial — but what could he do? He possessed no land and was a sojourner, passing through territory that belonged to others. In Genesis 23, we find Abraham negotiating with the inhabitants of the land where he was dwelling for a burial plot. In accordance with the rather long-winded but nevertheless well-mannered customs of the day, Abraham eventually purchased a field, containing a cave, in Hebron. It was "in the cave of the field of Machpelah before Mamre" (Gen.23:19) that Abraham was able to bury the body of Sarah.

If we continue reading Genesis, we reach the point where Abraham himself died "in a good old age, an old man, and full of years". His two sons, Isaac and Ishmael, buried him in the same grave as Sarah, "in the cave of Machpelah" (Gen.25:8,9). However, a new phrase appears at this point in the sacred text. We are told that when Abraham died, he "was gathered to his people" (Gen.25:8). This expression cannot refer to his burial, for as far as we know only Sarah had been buried in that cave. "His people" were not in the cave! While his body was given a decent burial, his *soul* was "gathered to his people". Who were "his people"? They were the people of faith; so the soul of Abraham, at his death, joined these believers who were already in the presence of God. His soul departed to the *heavenly* country that we have been considering in Hebrews 11.

The expression is also used in connection with the subsequent deaths of Isaac and Jacob. We learn that Isaac "died, and was gathered unto his people, being old and full of days" (Gen.35:29). His twin sons, Esau and Jacob, buried him. The earthly location is the same, and so is the heavenly. It was "to his people" that Isaac was gathered. His soul joined the souls of Abraham and Sarah, his parents, in the heavenly country. A few more years passed, and old age came upon Jacob too. Before dying, he instructed his sons to carry his mortal remains from Egypt (where he had been living) to Canaan. His great desire was to be buried with his ancestors in the same cave, where his grandparents, his parents, and his own wife (Leah) had been buried. In death, Jacob "was gathered unto his people" (Gen.49:33) and rejoined, in spirit, those who had passed on before him.

This is the dawning of the truth that we are considering. These Old Testament believers *had* a future! The people of God who have died live on in His presence! Having established this foundation, we can now move on and see how certain new features can be added to the Old Testament picture that we are painting.

Truth's Development

Throughout the Old Testament, death is referred to as *sleep*. Job's sufferings are proverbial, and very early in the book that bears his name, Job expresses the wish that he might have died at birth. If only he had escaped this life, he would have "lain still and been quiet"! "I should have slept," he declared, "then had I been at rest." Death is the mighty leveller; in its cold embrace he would have "slept" with kings, counsellors, and princes (Job 3:13—15). There is a finality about death, for "man lieth down, and riseth not: till the heavens be no more, they shall not awake, nor be raised out of their sleep" (Job 14:12). According to Job, death is "the house appointed for all living" (Job 30:23). What a silent house that must be! "The dead praise not the LORD, neither any that go down into silence" (Ps.115:17).

A little phrase is used repeatedly in the records of the kings of Israel and Judah. The phrase "slept with his fathers" first appears in 1 Kings 2:10 and refers to David. In the Authorized (King James) Version, this phrase is used to describe good kings as well as evil kings. Clearly, "slept with his fathers, and was buried …" relates to the body, and not to the spirit. The *body* of David is therefore pictured in death as appearing to be asleep. This explains the earlier references that Job made to death. When he spoke of "sleep" and being "silent" he was referring to the body, recumbent and still, and not to the soul. (More will be said about this later.)

Solomon, David's son, declared in Ecclesiastes 9:5 that "the dead know not anything". He also said that a man is no better than a beast, for "all go unto one place" (Eccl.3:19,20). Some have used such verses to support the idea that an unbeliever passes into oblivion and ceases to exist after death, but one vital fact is ignored by those who promote this view. Ecclesiastes is written from an "under the sun" perspective. This phrase (first used in 1:3) is important to grasp. It does not explain things *beyond* the sun, only *under* the sun. From a purely human perspective, a dead man and a dead dog have much in common. The cold, lifeless body can do nothing in this world. It exists in silence, with all powers of communication gone. One is no better off than the other. The bodies of both man and dog will decompose. *As far as this world is concerned*, the body sleeps. It can no longer respond to any terrestrial stimuli.

A second fact, evident in the Old Testament, is that death means *separation*. Job refers to life's rapid movement and the parting *from* this life that occurs at death. "My days are swifter than a weaver's shuttle, and are spent without hope," he lamented. How quickly that shuttle flew across the tapestry; and, sadly, there was nothing at the end to show for all the effort! Death faced Job, and those who could see him as he spoke *then* would see him no more. He makes the profound statement that, when one has died, "his place [shall not] know him any more" (Job 7:6—10). The fact is patently obvious. You may associate a particular individual with a certain place. The man is often seen in the garden; the lady can be seen sitting by the window. But when death strikes, they are *gone*. Never again will they be seen in that familiar earthly place.

Sometimes death can be a cause for rejoicing. Zophar, one of Job's friends, reminds us that "the triumphing of the wicked is short, and the joy of the hypocrite but for a moment". Though he may have enjoyed success and fame throughout his life, the time shall come when he will "fly away as a dream, and shall not be found". Again, we read that "neither shall his place any more behold him" (Job 20:5—9). Think of a tyrant who cruelly oppressed the citizens of his land. When he dies, there is a *separation*. He has gone from the country, and those who suffered under his misrule are free! Job himself makes it clear that at death "I go whence I shall not return," — even if it is "to the land of darkness and the shadow of death" (Job 10:21). Yes, it is clear from the Old Testament that at the moment of death there is *separation*, and life continues on earth without the one who has passed away.

A third fact can be considered. Some verses in the Old Testament make us aware of death's *sweetness*. Psalm 116:15 states, "Precious in the sight of the LORD is the death of his saints." Our view of death is therefore not altogether gloomy! It is a "precious" thing when the Lord calls His people into His presence — precious to Him, that is. (We shall return to this verse in the next chapter.) The psalmist wrote, "But God will redeem my soul from the power of the grave: for he shall receive me" (Ps.49:15). Notice here the *development* of truth. The grave *has* power over the body, but it has *no power* over the soul. The believer can look *beyond* the grave! The Lord will deliver His people and bring them into His eternal presence.

This point prepares us for the fourth observation. For the believer, there is *superiority* in death. A rather unusual incident is recorded in 1 Samuel 28. King Saul had lost contact with the Lord and was desperate for a divine message. Samuel, the prophet, had died, and Saul felt very much alone. What could he do? Saul decided to do something very foolish. He disguised himself and went to visit a medium, asking her to bring up Samuel from the dead. The Bible warns of the danger of dabbling with the occult and actually forbids the practice. A medium can make contact with evil spirits that impersonate dead souls, thus causing a person to believe that they are actually communicating with one who has departed. In this case "the witch of En-dor" (as she is known) "cried with a loud voice" when the figure appeared. It would seem that it *was* Samuel, for he spoke of being "disquieted" in having been brought back (1 Sam.28:15). The shock caused (both to Saul as well as to the medium) strongly suggests that Samuel *did* make a brief reappearance. If he was "disquieted" by his visit, it implies that Samuel had been in another realm that was far more pleasant. Connect this with the closing words of Psalm 16. Beyond the "corruption" of the grave is "the path of life". It is also plainly stated, "In thy presence is fulness of joy; at thy right hand there are pleasures for evermore" (Ps.16:11). Life beyond death evidently can be far better than the life we know now.

There are also references in the book of Psalms to "the house of the LORD." David, in his much-loved psalm, anticipated dwelling there "for ever" (Ps.23:6). In another psalm he also expressed a longing to "dwell in the house of the LORD all the days of my life" and "to behold the beauty of the LORD" (Ps.27:4). Those dwelling in that favoured abode "will be still praising thee" (Ps.84:4). These verses reveal to us something better than what can normally be experienced now.

In pursuing the development of this truth, a fifth point can be made. Death raises a mood of *seriousness*. Job reminds us that "the wicked is reserved to the day of destruction" and will "be brought forth to the day of wrath" (Job 21:30). We dare not treat such warnings lightly! A young man is warned by Solomon that "God will bring thee into judgment" (Eccl.11:9). In fact, "God shall bring every work into judgment, with every secret thing, whether it be good, or whether it be evil" (Eccl.12:14). It is sobering to realize that nothing escapes His gaze. Beyond death, lies judgment. We certainly need to tread carefully.

Death is not the end. Daniel was informed that resurrection follows death. For some it will be "to everlasting life", while for others it will be "to shame and everlasting contempt" (Dan.12:2). Daniel, as a believer who trusted in God, could look forward to "the end" when he would "stand in [his] lot at the end of the days" (Dan.12:13). We thought earlier about the concept of eternity being placed in the heart of man. Both "everlasting life" and "everlasting contempt" can be found beyond this life. Which is it to be? These verses demonstrate plainly the *seriousness* of death.

Truth's Destination

Where are these thoughts leading us? What lies ahead? Before bringing this chapter to its close, two points can be noted. First, there is *light beyond death*. An interesting verse is found in the book of Job. Thinking of the many things that God can do, Job declared, "He discovereth deep things out of darkness, and bringeth out to light the shadow of death" (Job 12:22). The darkness may hide many things from our sight, but the eye of God can penetrate the blackest midnight and bring into the light those things that are hidden from our view. To us, death is encompassed by shadows. But God can bring even "the shadow of death" into the light and show it up for what it is.

At the end of Job's book, we find the Lord questioning His servant. Job had spoken much and had boldly expressed many opinions, but what did he *really* know? Could he explain the origin of the universe or the wonders of Creation? "Have the gates of death been opened unto thee?" the Lord asked, "or hast thou seen the doors of the shadow of death?" (Job 38:17). The Lord was speaking of something He knew well but which was foreign to Job. To the human mind, the "gates of death" are firmly closed. We have no way of opening those gates or of exploring what lies beyond them. As for "the doors of the shadow of death" mentioned by the Almighty, we would not even know of their existence. They are invisible to us, but God who "is light" (1 Jn.1:5) can reveal them to us. He is able to dispel the shadows!

A second fact to note is that there is *life beyond death.* We can recall the familiar words of Psalm 23:6: "Surely goodness and mercy shall follow me all the days of my life: and I will dwell in the house of the LORD for ever." All through life the "goodness" and "mercy" of God pursue us; His blessings are unnumbered. But what lies *beyond* "the days of my life"? The little conjunction "and" opens up an eternal prospect. With certainty, the believer in the LORD can say, "I will dwell in His house for ever". Beyond *this* life is life everlasting! A few other verses could be considered, but one will suffice at this point. Asaph wrote, "Thou shalt guide me with thy counsel, and afterward receive me to glory" (Ps.73:24). That "glory" is to be found in heaven (Ps.73:25). Earlier in this chapter we considered the fact that God is the Guide of His people "even unto death" (Ps.48:14). But this verse takes us further. Beyond this life is *glory*! In other words, life of a far superior kind can be found beyond the gates of death.

"When the mists have rolled away ..."

In her nineteenth-century hymn, Annie H. Barker referred to that future day when the mists shall have rolled away. When those mists have been dispelled, the once-hidden landscape can be revealed. In the Old Testament period mists certainly prevailed, and the sight of God's people was obscured. Nevertheless, we *do* have some glimpses there of what lies ahead. With the fuller revelation of truth in the New Testament, those early mists did roll away. We now know so much more than the people of God knew in Old Testament times. But to understand *life beyond the sunset* it is important that we begin

13

with the Old Testament canvas — and especially with Abraham who longed for that "better country", a "heavenly" one (Heb.11:16). Like him, we ought to be people whose focus is on the city that has been founded by God Himself.

Chapter 2
Focal Points

There is a land of pure delight,
Where saints immortal reign;
Infinite day excludes the night,
And pleasures banish pain.

There everlasting spring abides,
And never-withering flowers;
Death, like a narrow sea, divides
This heavenly land from ours.

Sweet fields beyond the swelling flood
Stand dressed in living green;
So to the Jews old Canaan stood,
While Jordan rolled between.

Could we but climb where Moses stood,
And view the landscape o'er,
Not Jordan's stream, nor death's cold flood,
Should fright us from the shore.

Isaac Watts

In the first chapter we pictured the unequalled perfection of a sunset over the open sea on a clear evening, and we remarked on the way that such a scene can bring far-reaching thoughts into our minds. Darkness gradually creeps upon us as the light of day slowly fades into twilight. Another day has disappeared from our lives. Time's inexorable march continues with its unyielding regularity.

LIFE BEYOND THE SUNSET

Sunset can, effectively, be compared to the end of life. Henry Francis Lyte captures this mood in his meditative hymn *Abide with me*. He writes of the eventide falling fast, of the darkness deepening, and of "life's little day" ebbing out so swiftly. However, we must not imagine that life is something like a play acted out upon the stage. It is not as though a manager backstage can call "curtains!" with finality, and that is that. The sun may set upon our lives on earth, but there *is* life beyond the setting sun. Just as the sun never stops shining, so life continues; and if our life in this sphere ends, it will only continue in another realm.

God, in His Word, has made known to us what lies beyond the sunset. In the Bible we discover a progressive revelation, with more being revealed in the New Testament than in the Old Testament. We have likened the atmosphere of the Old Testament to being in a mist. Those who lived during Old Testament times could not see the future clearly. It was as though their view was obstructed by a dense mist.

The truth about life after death dawned with Abraham. By faith "he looked for a city which hath foundations, whose builder and maker is God" (Heb.11:10). He desired "a better country" than the one in which he lived or the one from which he had been called. He knew that God had "prepared for [him] a city" (Heb.11:16). When he died, we are told distinctly that he "was gathered to his people" (Gen.25:8). His soul left his body at death and joined the people of faith who had already entered the presence of God.

We have traced the development of this truth in the Old Testament as we considered the afterlife. It is clear that, in death, the body is pictured as *sleeping*. The expression is used a number of times in connection with the kings of Israel and Judah who "slept with their fathers" when they died. A supine body may be dead or may simply be sleeping. Some will readily admit that the slumbering body with an open mouth, discovered in a comfortable chair and enjoying an after-dinner nap, is not a very pretty sight!

Death can also be viewed in terms of *separation*. Job reminds us that the place that we have known on earth knows us no more when we have passed on (Job 7:10). It may have been a place that you were very much associated with, but when you have died you are not seen in that earthly place any more. It is an unarguable fact that you do not return to it. David expressed his awareness of this when his infant son died. He stated plainly that he would go to the child when he died, but the child would not return to him (2 Sam.12:23). Death spells out separation from life as we know it here, but death is not the end. It simply signals the beginning of life in another realm — or, we might say, the continuation of our lives elsewhere.

The Old Testament also makes us aware of the *sweetness* of death for the believer. (We are going to explore this theme further in this present chapter.) We find that it is possible to say with assurance, "God will redeem my soul from the power of the grave" (Ps.49:15). There is also a wonderful *superiority* about death, because those who die as believers enter the presence of the Lord where "pleasures for evermore" exist (Ps.16:11). However, there is a *serious* fact that must never be ignored. Beyond death is judgment, for we are all accountable to our Creator.

In our previous study we considered the *destination* of this truth. Where does it actually lead us? We have been brought to see that there is *light* beyond death, as well as *life*. The murky shadows of death have been brought into the light by the Lord (Job 12:22). Perhaps we are becoming aware that certain objects *can* be seen through the mist in the Old Testament. Imagine again that mist-filled valley which was described in the previous chapter. Depending upon the height to which the mist rises, it may be possible to see the tops of a few taller objects in the valley. Perhaps the highest branches of a particularly tall tree or a lofty church spire may just be visible, breaking through the top of the mist. The sight of such objects can give us clues about what may be found in the valley. Something similar can be discovered in the Old Testament. There are a few verses (not many) that seem to rise above the level of the mist and introduce us to truths that are developed more fully in the New Testament. In this chapter we are going to look at these "focal points" that resemble half a dozen tall, isolated trees growing in the valley, just visible above the level of the mist. These six verses are going to be divided into three groups so that we look at the verses in pairs.

Individual Perception

Thine eyes shall see the king in his beauty: they shall behold the land that is very far off.
Isaiah 33:17

Precious in the sight of the LORD is the death of his saints.
Psalm 116:15

Isaiah 33:17 is a real Old Testament gem that gives the people of God *reassurance*. We need to understand, first of all, the context in which the verse is set. Its true significance will be lost if this is ignored.

King Hezekiah was being oppressed by the Assyrians. Silver from the temple in Jerusalem had been sent to Assyria to pay the tribute demanded of Hezekiah, and the king was being mocked by the Assyrians for having trusted in Egypt. An aggressive message was proclaimed by an Assyrian envoy, who intended to undermine the people's confidence and belittle their good king before their eyes. The situation was grim, and Hezekiah "rent his clothes, and covered himself with sackcloth" before proceeding to the house of the Lord (2 Kings 19:1). It was indeed "a day of trouble, and of rebuke" (2 Kings 19:3).

Bleak though things appeared, the Lord had not abandoned His people. Through His prophet Isaiah, the Lord addressed the discouraged people of Judah, but first there was something to say to the Assyrians. For them, it was a message of woe. They had spoiled others, though they had not been spoiled themselves; their dealings with others had been treacherous, even though others had not dealt treacherously with them. The time was fast approaching when they would receive a just recompense. The Lord would arise from His throne and come to the aid of His maligned people (Isa.33:1;10).

The people of Judah must have been greatly comforted by the message of Isaiah. Instead of viewing their king clothed in sackcloth, they would view him "in his beauty" again, dressed in his royal robes. Hezekiah had been confined by the Assyrians, and his freedom had been greatly restricted. The situation was about to change dramatically. The king and people would, instead, see the land spread out before them — all of it — without having to be confined by the enemy any more (Isa.33:17).

However, the verse can also be interpreted in another way. There is a strong Messianic theme running through Isaiah. "Behold, a king shall reign in righteousness," declares the prophet (Isa.32:1). This is none other than the Lord Jesus Christ! Many Bible commentators see references to Him in Isaiah 33:17. Hezekiah, in his day, only foreshadowed the One who is to come. Believers on the Lord Jesus Christ love to see Him prefigured in this verse. He is "the King in his beauty"! Robes of glory adorn Him, and He is crowned with many crowns! What can be said about "the land that is very far off"? Surely this can be applied to heaven. Sometimes heaven *does* seem "very far off" from us. The trials of life can drag us down, and we can suffer for the cause of Christ. Many true Christians today are victimized and downtrodden simply because they *are* Christians. The words of this verse offer comfort and wonderful *reassurance*. "Thine eyes shall see the king in his beauty: they shall behold the land that is

19

very far off" (Isa.33:17). Let there be no doubt! If you belong to the Lord, you *will* see Him one day with your own eyes. Although heaven seems distant, you *will* view the "land of pure delight" that captivated the mind of Isaac Watts in his beautiful hymn. The certainty expressed in this verse needs to be impressed upon our hearts.

The prospect for the Christian is truly wonderful — but how will it be realized? How shall we be able to view the King of kings and the heavenly country? The other verse quoted earlier in the chapter provides the answer. "Precious in the sight of the LORD is the death of his saints" (Ps.116:15). Our reception on the other side of "the gates of death" (Job 38:17) will bring us into His presence. Death is not the enemy that we might fear! It is actually a "precious" experience because it will bring us to heaven. Why can it be described as "precious"? We must notice carefully that it is the death of *His saints* that is being considered. These are not just any people. These are the ones who have taken "the cup of salvation, and [called] upon the name of the LORD" (Ps.116:13). It is these people, and these alone, who discover that death is something "precious" to anticipate. Like the writer of this psalm, they can declare, "I love the LORD, because he hath heard my voice" (Ps.116:1).

Death is not the means of bringing every person to heaven. The only people who can look forward to entering "the land that is very far off" are those who are *saved*. It is vital to trust the Lord Jesus Christ ("the King" we have been considering) who died upon the cross for our sins. He offers us salvation from sin, but we must *take* the salvation that He offers by calling on His name. Have you ever prayed to Him in true sincerity and said, "Lord, please save me"? Are you able to say, "I really do believe that Jesus died for me"? If you have received His free gift of salvation, you will *love* Him for the sacrifice that He made for you at the cross. You will also understand that He has an infinite love for you and longs to bring you into the heavenly country where you will see Him. Death is *precious* for the believer, because it enables us to see the Lord in His beauty and to behold that land of pure delight.

If only we could catch a glimpse of the land that Isaac Watts describes! It is a land where "everlasting spring abides" because it lies beyond the chilling clutch of death. The "landscape" of heaven must be beyond compare! Truly, if we *were* able to catch a glimpse of heaven from where we are now, in much the same way that Moses was able to view the Promised Land from Mount Nebo, the wonder of that vision would banish all fear of death from us! In the words of the hymn, death is but "a narrow sea" which separates us from the heavenly country. What a prospect awaits the believer! *Individual perception* is guaranteed. Those who love the Lord *shall* see Him in His beauty and will behold the land that is promised to us.

Individual Perfection

But the path of the just is as the shining light, that shineth more and more unto the perfect day.
Proverbs 4:18

Thou shalt guide me with thy counsel, and afterward receive me to glory.
Psalm 73:24

God's people are described in Scripture as righteous, or "just". We can only be declared righteous through believing in the Lord (Gen.15:6) and accepting what He has done for us. For those who have been declared "just" by Him, a "path" to tread has been marked out. According to Proverbs 4:18, that path is like "the shining light". God Himself "is light" (1 Jn.1:5), and His light shines upon the pathway that He has revealed in His Word. That pathway is not simply to be observed. It is to be approached and entered, and progress should characterize the life of the child of God. How can we

21

make *headway* along the course that He has marked? We need to be advancing in the things of God, but how can this be done?

Psalm 73:24 provides an answer to these questions. The words "Thou shalt guide me with thy counsel" are significant. "Counsel" is available for the course that lies ahead. God wants His children to receive wisdom and direction from Him, and such "counsel" is never unavailable because the Lord is always with us. The previous verse declares, "Nevertheless I am continually with thee: thou hast holden me by my right hand" (Ps.73:23). In the difficulties and perplexities of life, we need to draw near to the Lord and ask Him to guide us in the decisions that we must make. With His guidance, it will be possible to make headway along "the path of the just" as He directs us according to the precepts of His Word.

In the New Testament, Paul spoke of leaving childhood behind and of becoming a man. Maturity is connected with seeing "face to face" and knowing more fully than we can know at the present time (1 Cor.13:11,12). What lies ahead of us? If we focus upon the *horizon*, what can we see? Proverbs 4:18 refers to "the perfect day" when there will be fulness of light. The darkness will then have passed, and the light will be shining without any hindrance. It may also cause us to think of a day that has no end. We are to tread the heavenly pathway looking ahead to the horizon and to the "perfect day" that is promised.

"Thou shalt guide me with thy counsel, and afterward receive me to glory" (Ps.73:24). Think of that! We are promised that God will guide us through life, and "afterward" receive us to glory. When our brief lives on earth are over, we have the prospect of entering a place of majesty and splendour. What glories lie before the child of God! Those who belong to the Lord are destined to share in His eternal glory! Well may we give thanks to God the Father who has fitted us to share in His inheritance, by making us saints and bringing us into

22

the light (Col.1:12). We are moving on towards these things, and we can look forward to the time when we shall be changed and receive the *individual perfection* promised in Holy Scripture to all who believe. (Such "perfection" is, of course, unattainable in our life on earth because of sin. Only the Lord can make us perfect, and that work is *future*.) He will change us in such a way that we will be equipped to live in the light of the "perfect day" that lies before us.

Individual Persuasion

For I know that my redeemer liveth, and that he shall stand at the latter day upon the earth: and though after my skin worms destroy this body, yet in my flesh shall I see God: whom I shall see for myself, and mine eyes shall behold, and not another...
Job 19:25—27

As for me, I will behold thy face in righteousness: I shall be satisfied, when I awake, with thy likeness.
Psalm 17:15

When we consider the pessimistic background against which the book of Job is set, the verses quoted above present a striking contrast. "For I know that my Redeemer liveth," Job declared. Yes, he had One who would take his side and plead his cause. He had longed for a mediator who could stand between him and God (9:33) and resolve the difficulties that existed. The need had been met, and a "redeemer" had been found. With great confidence, and yet with thankfulness, Job expressed his assurance that the Redeemer was living and would, in the future, set foot upon the earth.

What an outstanding verse this is, rising above all the mists that have filled that Old Testament valley! Job was fully persuaded of these things and was filled with *confidence*. We, in this twenty-first century, can share his confidence. The Redeemer is none other than Jesus Christ who died upon the cross. *He* lives again, having triumphed over death. We know from the promises of His Word that *He* shall "stand at the latter day upon the earth". Throughout the New Testament we can read promises that Job knew nothing of. We can be sure that our Redeemer *will* return and stand upon our planet again!

But Job does not only speak about his Redeemer. He also has something to say about himself. He knew that he would share in mankind's common lot. Death lay before him, and the body in which he had suffered would decompose in the grave and become, as Shakespeare bluntly wrote in Hamlet, *the food of worms*. Yet, some time after his departure from this life, Job was confident that his body would be raised from death. He is not speaking of reincarnation here but of resurrection. *Even though* worms might destroy his mortal frame, Job could affirm that "in my flesh shall I see God" (Job 19:26). This statement is not about a spirit being seeing God, or about being reconstituted into some other form of life. Job is emphatic that in his own flesh, as a resurrected person, he would see God. The words "whom I shall see for myself ... and not another" (v.27) confirm that this is the correct interpretation.

We can share this confidence that Job had because we have the added benefit of the New Testament to confirm what will happen. Beyond death we *shall* see the Lord. At the moment of death we pass, in spirit, into His presence. But when the Lord comes to summon the *bodies* of the dead from their graves, we shall be raised; and it is in our resurrected "flesh" that we shall see God for ourselves. The *individual persuasion* that was Job's can be ours too.

The other verse quoted at the head of this section adds to the picture that we are painting. Again, it is very *personal*. David writes, "As for me ..." (Psalm 17:15). Others may come and go, and the philosophies of men may change from one generation to the next. David was steadfast in his ambition and was assured that it would be realized. "I will behold thy face in righteousness," he declared. As we have pointed out before, we cannot make ourselves righteous; only God can make us righteous. This is done through the work of His own Son, and by Him *alone*. Having been made righteous by God, David knew that he was qualified to see the Lord's face, the face of the One whom Job called his "Redeemer". Again, if we are saved through the work of the Lord Jesus, we can make these words our own too. Faith, one day, will give place to *sight*. We shall behold His face.

This lovely confession also expresses *satisfaction*. "I shall be satisfied, when I awake, with thy likeness" (Ps.17:15). Does this mean that I shall be satisfied when I see what He actually looks like? That fact cannot be denied, but it is not the true meaning of the verse. "I shall be satisfied … with thy likeness" can only mean that I shall be satisfied when I resemble Him. Can such a thing possibly happen? Romans 8:29 affirms that it will, because God's purpose is that His people should "be conformed to the image of his Son". When the "dream" of this life is over, we shall awake in the presence of the Lord and discover that we have been made like Him. We shall bear His "image" and reflect Him perfectly. This is the hope of the Christian. Christ-likeness is our goal; our bodies shall be raised from the dust of death and fashioned anew. We shall see Him, and we shall be like Him.

Focal Points

What wonderful focal points these are, rising above the mists of the Old Testament! An individual *perception* of "the King" and of "the land" is promised in Isaiah 33:17. *Perfection* of the individual is also assured, for we shall enter the "perfect day" of Proverbs 4:18. As we ponder these amazing prospects, we can share the *persuasion* that Job and David had as individuals. We "know" that the Redeemer lives, and we can say, "I will behold His face". No doubts need remain in our minds.

LIFE BEYOND THE SUNSET

In Pilgrim's Progress, John Bunyan supplies a fitting verse with which we can conclude this chapter. As he journeyed towards the Promised Land, Christian (the pilgrim in the story) was shown the wonders of what the Lord had done. Moved by what he had seen, he broke forth with the following words of praise:

> "Where am I now? Is this the love and care
> Of Jesus, for the men that pilgrims are,
> Thus to provide! That I should be forgiven,
> And dwell already the next door to heaven!"

The Lord has certainly done great things for His people. Actually, we *are* already "next door to heaven"! We shall see Isaac Watts' "Land of pure delight, where saints immortal reign" — the land where "pleasures banish pain" and all is serene. Although it may sometimes appear to be "very far off", in another sense it could hardly be closer! Let us long for it more than we do and seek to tread in "the path of the just" as we move onward towards the perfect eternal day.

Chapter 3

The City of God

There is a city bright,
Closed are its gates to sin;
Naught that defileth,
Naught that defileth,
Can ever enter in.

Lord, make me, from this hour,
Thy loving child to be;
Kept by Thy power,
Kept by Thy power,
From all that grieveth Thee.

Saviour, I come to Thee!
O Lamb of God, I pray,
Cleanse me and save me,
Cleanse me and save me,
Wash all my sins away.

Till in the snowy dress
Of Thy redeemed I stand,
Faultless and stainless,
Faultless and stainless,
Safe in that happy land!

Mary A.S. Deck

We have seen already that in the Old Testament we are not told very much about the life to come. Just here and there, in a few places, we are given a glimpse of what lies before us and of the life that exists beyond the setting sun. Proverbs 4:18 speaks of "the path of the just" which grows ever brighter until the perfect day dawns. A believer who leaves this life does not go out into the darkness! Rather, he goes out into the light! Job had tremendous assurance of these things. "I know that my Redeemer liveth!" he cried with great conviction. Even though his body might rot in the grave, he knew that it would one day be raised from the sleep of death, and he knew that in his flesh he would see God (Job 19:25—27). David wrote similar words in Psalm 17:15, for when he "awoke" in the next life he would be satisfied with the Lord's own likeness. He would, one day, be like Him.

Abraham, you may recall, was looking for a city built by God Himself (Heb.11:10). Indeed, God has prepared a city for those who are the people of faith (Heb.11:16). In this chapter we shall develop the theme of the *City of God*.

What do we know about this city? From the Old Testament, we know very little. Abraham seems to have known of no more than its existence. Details were hidden from his view. From the New Testament we discover more — though we might wish that we knew a lot more than we are told! How often, when wanting to find answers, we turn to the writings of respected servants of God. What, for instance, did C. H. Spurgeon have to say about heaven? Among the many sermons preached by Mr. Spurgeon and recorded in print, we can find a number dealing with the life to come. A volume of sermons from Spurgeon's ministry has been compiled, entitled *The Father's House*. In one of these sermons, C. H. Spurgeon states: "It is very little that we can know of the future state, but we may be quite sure that we know as much as is good for us … If God wills us not to know, we ought to be satisfied not to know. Depend on it, He has told us all about heaven that is necessary to bring us there." [1] It could hardly have been put better than that!

Sometimes we are inquisitive and want to know more. Children may want to know more than is good for them and, recognizing this, their parents may decide only to tell them as much as they *need* to know. The fact is that our Heavenly Father has told us all that *we* need to know. His Son, the Lord Jesus Christ, came to earth in order to make heaven known to us. On one or two occasions He pulled back the curtain, as it were, and showed us things that we could not have discovered by ourselves.

In this chapter we shall focus our attention upon two passages of

---

[1] *The Father's House*, by C. H. Spurgeon, Fox River Press, Oswego, Illinois, 2002: p.302.

Scripture. In Revelation we learn a very important fact about *Entrance to the City*, while in Luke 16 we are made aware of the *Enjoyment of the City* by its inhabitants. This is the City of God to which Abraham referred.

Entrance to the City — Refused

And there shall in no wise enter into it any thing that defileth, neither whatsoever worketh abomination, or maketh a lie: but they which are written in the Lamb's book of life.
Revelation 21:27

Revelation 21 presents to us a city illuminated by the glory of God. The sun and moon which are part of our solar system, and upon which we depend so much, are not needed in a realm where the glory of God and the Lamb shine with celestial brightness. In olden times the gates of earthly cities were closed securely at night; but in the heavenly city the gates remain open permanently, for there is no night there (Rev.21:23&25). The closing verse of the chapter, however, makes an emphatic statement. "There shall in no wise enter into it any thing that defileth" (v.27). Although the gates remain open, they are somehow guarded. Holy standards dictate that nothing impure can ever enter the city.

I cannot read this verse without recalling that delightful children's story, *Christie's Old Organ*, written by Mrs. O. F. Walton[2]. I was presented with a copy of the book as a Sunday School prize many years ago, and I still have it in my possession. The story is about a poor old man named Treffy who owned a barrel-organ which he played in the city's streets in order to make a living. His favourite song was *Home sweet Home*. Christie was a raggedly-dressed little boy whose mother had died. Before her death she had told Christie that she was going "home" — which puzzled the young child.

---

[2] *Christie's Old Organ* by Mrs. O. F. Walton, Lutterworth Press, London: 1948.

One evening he crept up to the door of the dingy attic where old Treffy lived and listened to the music being played. A friendship developed between the two of them, but the old man became weak and ill and unable to take the barrel-organ out. Treffy finally yielded to Christie's pleading and allowed the boy to take the treasured instrument out and play it for him.

Treffy had only been given a month to live, and he began to realize that he must find out about heaven. He asked Christie to discover what he could, and the search resulted in the young boy attending a mission hall where the hymn *There is a city bright,* quoted at the beginning of this chapter, was sung. That hymn was the beginning of Christie's search which resulted in both he and old Treffy finding salvation in Christ.

The hymn begins:

> *There is a city bright, closed are its gates to sin;*
> *Naught that defileth, naught that defileth,*
> *Can ever enter in.*

Clearly Mary Deck was thinking of Revelation 21:27. Nothing impure or unclean can possibly enter the holy presence of God. The standards set are incredibly high. Nothing that causes what God considers to be an abomination, and nothing untrue, can enter His presence.

A comprehensive list can be found earlier in the same chapter. "The fearful, and unbelieving, and the abominable, and murderers, and whoremongers, and sorcerers, and idolaters, and all liars, shall have their part in the lake which burneth with fire and brimstone: which is the second death" (v.8). We might classify things differently and consider some of these practices to be more serious than others, but God is a perfect Being. As He is true, no liars can find a home in His august presence. Entrance to the city is refused: *by no means* shall anything that defiles appear before Him. All who are tainted by sin are kept outside.

Entrance to the City — Restricted

Only one class of people can enter the presence of God. Those whose names are found in the Lamb's book of life are the only ones who can enter — and no others (v.27). The idea of names being recorded is found elsewhere in Scripture. After the Lord Jesus had commissioned His larger band of followers to minister for Him, they returned from their period of service in great elation. "Even the evil spirits are subject to us, Lord," they announced. The Saviour exercised caution. They ought not to rejoice in what *they* had done but in the fact that their names were written in heaven (Lk.10:20).

In Revelation 3:5 a promise was made to the overcomer. "I will not blot out his name out of the book of life," the Lord declared. The "book of life" is also mentioned in Revelation 20. As well as His "books" in which humanity's deeds have been recorded, God has control of "the book of life". It is solemnly revealed that those whose names have not been recorded in that book will be "cast into the lake of fire" (Rev.20:12;15). What an awful prospect this is!

The "book" mentioned in Revelation 21:27, however, is specifically called "the Lamb's book of life". This takes us back, at once, to John 1:29. When he saw the Lord Jesus coming towards him, John the Baptist proclaimed, "Behold the Lamb of God, which taketh away the sin of the world." He knew that the thousands of lambs that had been offered upon Israel's altars for centuries had all prefigured the coming Saviour. The Lord Jesus would make future animal sacrifices for sin unnecessary after His once-for-ever sacrifice upon the cross. (See Heb.10:12.) God's own Son is central to Scripture and is its theme. In Revelation 5 He is seen in heaven as the one object of His people's praise. "Worthy is the Lamb," they declare, "to receive power, and riches, and wisdom, and strength, and honour, and glory, and blessing" (Rev.5:12). Why is He worthy of the praise? The answer is that by the shedding of His blood He has redeemed His people to God" (Rev.5:9). It is *His people* whose names have been recorded in that book of life.

It is interesting to compare this verse with Psalm 118. There we read, "Open to me the gates of righteousness: I will go into them, and I will praise the LORD: this gate of the LORD, into which the righteous shall enter" (Ps.118:19,20). The gates of the city are truly "gates of righteousness," and only those whom Christ declares righteous can enter through them. However, those whom He has fitted can indeed enter through those gates and joyfully "praise the LORD".

Consider again the touching words of Mary Deck's hymn. The individual must grasp the truth of Revelation 21:27 and be genuinely moved to repentance. The words of the second verse make a very fitting prayer:

> *Saviour, I come to Thee! O Lamb of God, I pray,*
> *Cleanse me and save me, cleanse me and save me,*
> *Wash all my sins away.*

Conscious of our guilt before a God who is more holy than we can ever understand, we must plead the merits of the Lord Jesus and ask to be cleansed from sin through His precious blood.

Those who have availed themselves of His work at Calvary can look ahead to the time when they will be in His presence, totally free from all trace of sin.

> *Till in the snowy dress of Thy redeemed I stand,*
> *Faultless and stainless, faultless and stainless,*
> *Safe in that happy land!*

Entrance to the city is definitely *restricted*. Only those who have had dealings with the Saviour and have received His pardon may enter the city. But, by His infinite grace, they have a "right" to enter through those gates into the city (Rev.22:14) where they will praise Him for evermore.

Enjoyment of the City

In Luke 16:19—31 we have an account, from the lips of the Lord Jesus, that opens up the future state for us. Many refer to this as "the parable" of the rich man and Lazarus, but there is evidence to suggest that this is not a parable at all. Familiar words such as "And He spake this parable unto them ..." (used in Luke 15:3 and elsewhere) are absent from this passage. In parables, generally speaking, the people that feature are not named. Here we are distinctly told of "a certain rich man" as if a particular individual was in the Saviour's mind. Events that have actually happened can be narrated, and this is most likely what we find here.

The fact that the incident refers to death, followed by torment, would make some prefer to classify it as a "parable". If this is *only* a parable, we need not concern ourselves too much with the details. However, matters are raised in the "story" that are confirmed elsewhere in the Bible, so it is only those who wish to sidestep the force of Holy Scripture who will relegate it to the realm of "parable" or even fantasy. No, the incident recounted in these verses is extremely instructive. We must accept it at face-value. Three "stages" can be viewed.

Before the Grave

The incident recounted by the Lord Jesus commences in this life *before* the grave. We are told of "a certain rich man" — a particular individual who may have been known to some of those listening to our Lord. The man was "clothed in purple" — which was what the wealthy would wear, and "fine linen" — which refers to undergarments which were made from special flax (v.19). He "fared sumptuously every day," living off the fat of the land and enjoying the best gourmet foods. Life, for him, was a constant round of pleasure and entertainment.

It is instructive to notice the context of this passage. The Lord Jesus had been addressing the Pharisees who loved money and justified themselves before men (v.14,15). The things that are valued highly by men are an abomination in God's sight. The Pharisees would have admired the rich man and would have seen his wealth as evidence of God's approval. The Lord's teaching here is a response to their viewpoint. The incident that follows demonstrates how very different God's approval was. In His estimation, the poor beggar was the more worthy character — though he would have been unaware of any worth in himself.

The other person described by the Lord Jesus could hardly have presented more of a contrast. He was a beggar — which literally means one who crouched or cowered as he begged. However, the words "a certain beggar named Lazarus" (v.20) alert us again to the fact that the Lord had a particular individual in mind. Surprisingly, the one who is named by Jesus is not the rich man but the beggar! Had the Pharisees been telling a story like this they would have named the rich man; but — as we have seen — God views things very differently.

The name Lazarus is significant too. It means "God is helper." Can we not imagine how he might have been mocked? "So God is your helper! There's not much sign of Him helping you, dirty beggar that you are!" Yet, as the story unfolds, we see that of the two *he* was the one who knew God as his helper.

"Full of sores" the poor beggar was cast down, like an unclean object, at the rich man's gate. It seemed a likely place to receive help from one who had so much. He longed for some "crumbs" of comfort from the rich man's table. Surely some leftovers from his ample supply of gourmet foods might find their way to him in all his need? His companions at the gate were the dogs; these were not the finely groomed family pets that we might think of today but wild scavengers that sought to satisfy their own appetites. Yet, although unclean, they did offer him more comfort than most human beings in that they "licked his sores" (v.21). Those disfigured and ulcerated limbs received some relief from his untamed companions, but the fact that they *did* lick his flesh proves to us that he was too weak to drive them away and not clothed sufficiently to prevent them having access to him.

What a contrast is presented as we look at these two individuals! Their lives *before the grave* could not have been more different.

Beyond the Grave

The second stage in the narrative takes us beyond the grave. After an unspecified time, "the beggar died, and was carried by the angels into Abraham's bosom" (v.22). What a surprise this must have been for the Pharisees! Abraham was considered to be the father of the faithful. Lazarus, the poor beggar, must have been a man of faith himself to be carried to where Abraham was.

But there is something very interesting and enlightening to observe in this verse. We know from Hebrews 1:14 that the angels of God are "ministering spirits" that serve His purposes and actually minister to the "heirs of salvation". Compare this verse with Psalm 34:7: "The angel of the LORD encampeth round about them that fear him, and delivereth them." Does this not suggest to us that at the moment of death, as God prepares to take one of His children away from earth, He sends one of His angels ("ministering spirits") to *deliver* that one from a life of pain and suffering? Some of God's dear children, in the moments immediately before death, have spoken of having seen angels hovering near.

"The rich man also died, and was buried" (v.22). We can picture an elaborate funeral taking place with glowing tributes and appreciations for one whose mark in life had been great. There is no mention of a burial in Lazarus' case. His poor emaciated body was probably flung into a common paupers' grave.

But the contrast continues and would have alarmed the Pharisees. After death the rich man found himself "in hell" [many other translations have *Hades*], a place of torment (v.23). Bible scholars frequently point out that this is the equivalent of *Sheol* in the Old Testament and means the place of the departed. It is not *Gehenna*, the lake of fire, known as hell. However, although *Hades* is not the *final* abode of the ungodly, it is still, nevertheless, a place of anguish. (Purgatory, it should be pointed out, has no biblical support.)

In torment after death, the rich man was able to lift up his eyes and see Abraham "afar off" with Lazarus beside him. He was not *with* Abraham, as the Pharisees might have supposed. Instead he could *see* Lazarus enjoying the company of Abraham. We might ask whether the rich man had ever "lifted up his eyes" before. His life had been thoroughly self-centred, and he never appeared to have lifted up his eyes to take notice of Lazarus while on earth.

The rich man cried out for help. "Father Abraham," he cried (though Abraham was not his father) "please send Lazarus to me with just a little cold water to quench my thirst, because I am tormented in this flame" (cf.v.24). Although his body lay in the grave and his sufferings in the place of the departed were therefore spiritual, the anguish is expressed in bodily terms in order that we might understand how he actually felt.

We might be inclined to feel sorry for the man. Perhaps he should have another chance, we may think. The fact remains that he had not changed. Although experiencing torment, he was *still* a selfish individual and could only think of his own discomfort being relieved and of Lazarus being the servant that could be sent to his aid. Significantly, too, he did not suggest being transferred from the place of torment to the place of bliss. Did he perhaps realize that he would not really have enjoyed Abraham's company?

Abraham, in his first response, instructed the rich man to "remember" certain things. The use of this word proves to us that memory remains beyond the grave. In his lifetime he had received his own good things (and there had been plenty of them!) while Lazarus had received "evil things" (v.25). Now it had all been reversed and the balance redressed: Lazarus was the one being comforted, while the rich man was tormented.

We must be clear that the rich man was not in a place of torment *because* he was rich. The Bible plainly tells us in Genesis 13:2 that Abraham himself was a rich man. The difference was that Abraham was not preoccupied with his wealth; with the rich man of Luke 16 a materialistic spirit had rendered faith irrelevant and unnecessary. A "great gulf" was also "fixed" between the two destinies (v.26). If anyone purposed to cross from one abode to the other, he would find it utterly impossible. The yawning chasm could *never* be bridged. Nobody could come from the place of bliss to the place of torment bringing relief, and it was equally impossible to escape from the place of torment and find refuge in the place of bliss.

The words of our Lord Jesus recorded here rule out completely the idea of purgatory. There is no place of suffering after death from which it is possible to escape, as some teach. The prayers of the saints for those who have departed, and deeds of kindness, are completely unable to deliver one from torment. The gulf is "fixed" — and so is the destiny. After death, if you find yourself in the place of torment, that is where you will remain. Conversely, those in that place of bliss after death will never lose the blessing of being associated with it. However, although the rich man could see Lazarus after death, we are not told that Lazarus caught sight of the rich man. From that place of blessedness it seems highly unlikely that a view of those in torment is possible.

Life for the believer now may be hard. There may be suffering and privation, pain and persecution. The poor beggar knew enough of that! But when the child of God arrives in His presence after death, all is bliss! The expression "Abraham's bosom" must refer to heaven. Let us be clear: those who die having trusted in Jesus Christ as their Saviour pass into His immediate presence. They are *comforted*. The shame and indignities experienced down here are over! The real *enjoyment* of the Lord's presence has begun! God's children will find themselves *with* Abraham (and close to him) in the city that had occupied his gaze.

Beside the Grave

The final stage in the narrative brings us back to earth, as it were, and we stand *beside* the grave. There is a very important lesson to learn. The rich man had a request to make, and initially it appears to be a caring suggestion. If Lazarus was not permitted to visit him in torment, perhaps it might be possible for him to be sent on a mission back to earth. The rich man had five brothers still living. Might it not be possible for Lazarus to be sent to them with a warning? However, the Greek text indicates that the rich man was still conscious of his position in life and addressed Abraham as an equal. He still thought of Lazarus as a servant who could be sent to others. It was vital, he reasoned, to warn them lest they should find themselves in torment with him.

Millions of obstinate and thoughtless souls today are in that place of torment where there is weeping and gnashing of teeth. If they could send a message to us, they would. The echoing voice from beyond the grave would say to those who are still lost, "Don't come here!

Avoid this place at all costs!" Can we be indifferent?

Abraham, however, refused the appeal. His reply, "They have Moses and the prophets: let them hear them" (v.29) may seem to us almost offhand. But the words of Abraham are stamped with divine approval. When He was faced by detractors, the Lord Jesus told them that He need not bring any accusation against them before the Father. Moses, who they claimed to trust, would be an adequate accuser. He continued, "For had ye believed Moses, ye would have believed me: for he wrote of me. But if ye believe not his writings, how shall ye believe my words?" (John 5:45—47). Moses lived long before Christ but prophesied of His coming. Within his writings are references to the coming Messiah. The Pharisees claimed to believe Moses, but as a matter of fact they did not. If they had *really* believed Moses they would have believed Christ, for He fulfilled the prophecies Moses had made. The Scriptures point to Christ and are the truth of God. We dismiss them at our own peril.

The rich man begged to differ. He attempted to convince Abraham that if a messenger from the dead visited his five brothers, they would "repent" — or change their minds (v.30). Abraham, however, had the final word. "If they hear not Moses and the prophets," he responded, "neither will they be persuaded, though one rose from the dead" (v.31). Such is the hardness of the human heart. Even a return visit from Lazarus would not persuade the wealthy man's five brothers. In other words, the written testimony of Moses in Holy Scripture was more compelling than a visit that might be made by Lazarus. Talk of someone appearing from the dead could be explained away and dismissed. As we know, a more powerful witness than Lazarus *has* been raised from the dead. When our Lord Jesus Christ was raised on Easter Sunday a story was concocted by the authorities that His disciples had stolen the body. That story gained credence, and still today His resurrection is dismissed as a fanciful idea.

Fixed

We have seen from this account that after death it is too late to change your location. The great gulf that is fixed prevents movement between the two contrasting destinies after death. We need to ensure that we are heading for the right one. As the message of the gospel goes out, the *welcome* is coupled with a *warning*. We must flee from the wrath to come. None of us deserve to enter the City of God, but if we come to Jesus Christ and sincerely ask Him to forgive our sins and take control of our lives we can be assured of an entrance one day. I urge you to receive Christ as your personal Saviour if you have never done so.

For the rich man of Luke 16, the gates of the city remained closed. He was shut out for ever. Lazarus experienced something entirely different. God truly *was* his "helper" as his name had suggested! The angels carried him within the gates to a place where he experienced eternal *comfort*. For all believers today there is "comfort" to be found in the face of death, according to 1 Thessalonians 4:18. The Lord is coming again, and the bodies of those who have died will be raised. The only ones who enter the City of God are those whose names are recorded in the Lamb's book of life (Rev.21:27). Abraham, by faith, looked ahead to Christ's day and rejoiced (Jn.8:56). That patriarch is now in the presence of the Lord, and those who die believing in Jesus pass into His presence too. Though we may miss them, we would not wish them back because their sufferings in this world are over and they have entered the eternal city where, according to Psalm 16:11, there is fulness of joy and pleasures exist for evermore.

Chapter 4

<u>The Father's Home</u>

Bright home of our Saviour, what glories await
The spirits that pass through thy bright, pearly gate!
What anthems of rapture, unceasing and high,
Compose the loud chorus that gladdens the sky!
Home! Home! Sweet, sweet home!
Prepare me, dear Saviour, for yonder blest home.

The home of the ransomed, the land of the blest;
Where pilgrims shall enter a glorious rest,
Shall wander in gladness through pastures of green,
And drink the still waters of pleasures serene.

The home that our Saviour has gone to prepare —
No heart can conceive of the blessedness there;
Of raptures unending awaiting the just
When pure in His likeness they rise from the dust.

We bless Thee, dear Saviour, who call'st us to share
The beautiful home Thou hast gone to prepare;
We trust in Thy mercy that, washed from our sin,
Through yonder bright gates we may all enter in.

Anon

The Word of God makes it very clear that this life is not everything. There *is* a life to come, a life beyond this present sphere. When the sun above us sets, *our* day is over; but light continues out to the west of us where the sun is still shining. People there are still enjoying the hours of daylight. In much the same way, spiritually speaking, when the sun goes down upon your life or mine, there *is* life beyond the sunset.

41

This truth can only be faintly discerned in the Old Testament. We are not told many things there about the life to come, though Abraham knew of it and looked for a city whose Builder and Maker is God (Heb.11:10). Job knew that after death he would be raised to see God (Job 19:26). Asaph was assured that when this life was over he would be received to glory (Ps.73:24). These glimpses make us long to know more, and in the New Testament a much fuller revelation is given of the life that continues beyond the sunset.

In our previous chapter we compared two men in Luke 16. One of them had lived as a beggar, but when he died he found himself with Abraham in a place of bliss. The other was a rich man who had every material comfort he could possibly wish for in this life, but after death he found himself in a place of torment. It was the Lord Jesus who pulled the curtain aside, as it were, and revealed the future to us. The rich man was not condemned *because* of his wealth; the fact is that he was not a true child of Abraham.

In this chapter we are going to look at another revelation given by the Lord Jesus, this time found in John 14. We have already noticed that Abraham was seeking a heavenly country and a city that could not be found in this world. The book of Revelation presents that city to us. The city can only be entered by those whose names are recorded in the Lamb's book of life (Rev.21:27). In John 14 the Lord Jesus did not speak of a *country* or of a *city* but of a *house* — or, we might say, a *home*.

Before looking at His teaching in John 14, however, it is important to understand the mission that lay before the Lord Jesus. In John 5:24 He said, "He that heareth my word, and believeth on him that sent me, hath everlasting life, and shall not come into condemnation: but is passed from death unto life." From this verse, we learn that Jesus was *sent* into the world on a mission: He was sent by His Father. On many occasions He found Himself in conflict with the Pharisees. He told them plainly in John 7:33ff that He would only be with them for "a little while" before returning to His Father. The time would come when they would seek Him but be unable to find Him. It would also be impossible for them to follow Him where He was going. A little later, in John 8:21, He told them again that they would die in their sins and be unable to follow Him to His destination. What a terrible prospect lay before them — and how awful for *us* to die in our sins, too!

As we continue reading through John's gospel we find the Lord Jesus addressing a different group of people. The closing words in John 13 were addressed to His disciples. In similar fashion, He told them that He would only be with them for a little while longer. "As I said unto the Jews, Whither I go, ye cannot come: so now I say to you," He told them (Jn.13:33). Some deeply challenging instructions follow, as the Saviour gave "a new commandment" to His disciples that they should "love one another" with the same kind of love that He had displayed to them. The genuine love that they had for one another would clearly demonstrate to the world that they belonged to Him (Jn.13:34,35).

Simon Peter had a question: he wanted to know where the Lord was going. The answer he received was similar to the one given to the Jews (v.33), for Jesus said to him, "Whither I go, thou canst not follow me now; but thou shalt follow me afterwards" (Jn.13:36). The Saviour was going to leave them, and in due time they would follow Him. This provides the background to the wonderful passage before us concerning *The Father's Home*.

An evening visit to a large city can be very enlightening. The busy shoppers have gone home, and the streets are less congested; but the city is not deserted. A resident population begins to emerge. You will see some of them sitting on benches, while others can be found in shop doorways — some of them being quite young folk. They have cardboard, blankets, and perhaps a few possessions in plastic bags, and they are about to try and make themselves comfortable for the night. These are the homeless people who live out of doors on the streets in all weathers. Many of them will have heart-breaking stories to tell — perhaps of broken homes, of relationships that failed, or of how the city lights had attracted them but had proved a bitter disappointment. Addictions to drink or drugs may also have affected them. Not all, however, are young people. Many older folk will be found there too, some having experienced misfortune in life and others financial loss. But what is common to all of them, irrespective of their age or life history, is that they are homeless.

Very often those of us who have homes of our own do not appreciate them as much as we should. It is a great blessing to possess a home or to live in a place where care is experienced.

In this chapter, as we look at John 14:1—6, I want to take the simple word H-O-M-E and develop four thoughts from its letters.

The *Happiness* of that Home

You may be familiar with the expression, "An Englishman's home is his castle". A castle is, of course, a place of safety. The idea being expressed is that the typical Englishman is supposed to be safe within his home and to be in charge of it. He will want to enjoy being there and will only allow into his "castle" that which promotes his own happiness. We can understand this reasoning. Happiness is a precious commodity, but it can only exist when security prevails and anything that threatens is excluded.

My wife and I have happy memories of homes where we have stayed over the years. In fact, in our present home we have various items of furniture that used to be in some of those homes that we visited. Now, please do not misunderstand what I am saying. I am not asking you to feel sorry for us because we possess certain pieces of furniture that are second-hand! The items that came from family members who are no longer with us are treasured because of *memories* that are attached to them. Looking at an item of furniture that we inherited, we remember happy hours spent in the home where the furniture once stood.

Perhaps you can recall a home that you have loved to visit. If you can, I would suggest that the positive feelings within your heart are not because of the poshness or wealth that could be seen but because of the *atmosphere*. The outstanding quality of the home will have been the happy atmosphere, and the fact that you were made *welcome* there has not been forgotten.

Is heaven a place of happiness? Of course it is! "In thy presence is fulness of joy; at thy right hand there are pleasures for evermore" (Ps.16:11). David wrote of "the house of the LORD" in his psalms. He longed to "dwell in the house of the LORD all the days of [his] life" (Ps.27:4). It is as though David wanted to enjoy the atmosphere of that home every day that he lived on earth. He also knew that when life reached its close he would "dwell in the house of the LORD for ever" (Ps.23:6).

What a wonderful home it must be! There will be no unhappiness to spoil its pleasures. All tears will be wiped from sorrowful eyes, and there will be no more death, sorrow, crying, or pain (Rev.21:4). Some have complained about heaven and imagined that those who go there will spend most of their time sitting on clouds and playing harps. What nonsense! Such an idea is not found in the Bible!

Certainly there *will* be rejoicing in heaven. We have a preview of this in two parables recorded in Luke 15. Speaking of a shepherd's joy when one lost sheep from the flock of a hundred is found, the Lord Jesus declared, "Likewise joy shall be in heaven over one sinner that repenteth … " (Lk.15:7). In the other parable, where a woman swept the house and searched diligently until her missing piece of silver was found, He said, "Likewise … there is joy in the presence of the angels of God over one sinner that repenteth" (Lk.15:10). These verses assure us that heaven *is* a place of rejoicing and happiness. All sorrow will have been banished.

The *Otherness* of that Home

I have coined that word because it is important to understand that heaven is so different from what we know now. It cannot compare with any earthly home. In his hymn, *There's a Friend for little children*, Albert Midlane wrote:

> *No home on earth is like it,*
> *Nor can with it compare,*
> *For everyone is happy,*
> *Nor could be happier, there.* [3]

An elderly pastor dreaded dying and felt helpless to console others whose loved ones had experienced death. The time came when the pastor had to move house. After his furniture had been taken outside and placed in the removal vehicles, he lingered alone within the empty walls. He felt reluctant to leave. He had such happy memories of his own children growing up there many years before, and he recalled the precious times that he had spent with the Lord in his study. As he stood thoughtfully, a friend tapped him on the shoulder and said, "Pastor, your new home is better than this." A new home? Yes, he was going to a new home; and God used those words, he said later, to show him that he need not dread dying. Heaven is going to be so much better than any earthly home!

In John 14:1, Jesus said to His disciples: "Let not your heart be troubled." They *were* troubled, and perhaps they felt that they had good reason to be. The Lord Jesus had spoken of leaving them, and

---

[3] In passing I cannot miss the opportunity to say how much better it would be if children today were taught words like this. They are so different from many of the trashy and trendy songs and choruses that are sung nowadays and mean nothing!

they would be unable to follow Him (Jn.13:33). Simon Peter had expressed a determination to follow Christ, and was vehement in pledging his loyalty, but Jesus had warned the disciple of his own imminent denial (Jn.13:36—38). A little earlier, Jesus had solemnly told them that one member of the group would actually betray Him (Jn.13:21,22). They had looked, aghast, at one another. Who ever could it be? The Lord Jesus Himself was "troubled in spirit" (Jn.13:21), but there was no need for *them* to be troubled. That was why He spoke to them in the way that He did. "Let not your heart be troubled," He told them. "Ye believe in God, believe also in me." (Jn.14:1). As the Son of God, He could be trusted. He was telling them the truth.

The words that follow are a great comfort to God's children and offer unparalleled hope. "I go to prepare a place for you," the Saviour said; "and if I go and prepare a place for you, I will come again, and receive you unto myself; that where I am, there ye may be also" (Jn.14:2b,3). His departure from them was all part of His mission. Following His death at Calvary and subsequent resurrection, He would return to His Father in heaven. But at some future moment He would return *from* heaven in order to "receive" His people and bring them home.

When young children are told of a visit that is going to be made to a home that they love, their faces light up. In just the same way we should be overjoyed to think that our Saviour is coming to take us to our home above. What a place it is!
Mrs. J. A. Trench wrote:-

> *O what a home! But such His love*
> *That He must bring us there,*
> *To fill that home, to be with Him,*
> *And in His glory share.*
> *The Father's house, the Father's heart,*
> *All that the Son is given,*

Made ours, the objects of His love,
And He, our joy in heaven.

In order to enter that home, however, we will need to be changed —
and we shall be! We are told by the apostle Paul that because it is
impossible for "corruption" to "inherit incorruption" all God's
children will be changed and made fit for those eternal realms (1
Cor.15:50,51).

The *Magnificence* of that Home

Homes on earth are often too small! Many of us probably wish that
we had more space available. We may visit homes that feel rather
cramped; perhaps the furniture swamps the lounge, and there is very
little room to move around. Heaven is not like that! The expression
"many mansions" (Jn.14:2) implies that there is ample space.

The word translated as "mansions" in the Authorised Version could
also be rendered "abodes". It is found further on in the same chapter
where, in verse 23, it actually appears as "abode". The Lord Jesus
spoke of the one who loved and obeyed Him and promised that He
and His Father would come and make their "abode" with him. (To
use "mansion" in verse 23 would have been out of place: "we will
come ... and make our mansion with him.") In the Father's house are
many abodes, or dwelling places. Does the expression imply that
there will be separate apartments in heaven? There has been a lot of
conjecture as interested individuals have tried to "read into" the
simple expression. We would do best to take it at its face-value. All
that needs to be said is that our Saviour has personally prepared a
place for His children where there will be ample space for all who
believe. If we needed to understand things differently, He would
have told us (Jn.14:2).

What is heaven *really* like? Although the word "mansions" is not
used in newer Bible translations, it is not out of place. A *mansion*

48

suggests splendour and magnificence. Such a thought expresses heaven accurately, as we shall see.

In order to appreciate the splendour of the Father's home, we need to turn to Revelation 21. The apostle John's vision whets our appetite and shows us the glories associated with His presence. Although figurative language is certainly used and it may not be right to interpret everything literally, the passage *does* give us a good idea of what heaven is like. John, the apostle, was shown the "new Jerusalem, coming down from God out of heaven, prepared as a bride adorned for her husband" (Rev.21:2). What he saw, he describes in this verse as "the holy city". The vision was accompanied by a *voice*, for John heard "a great voice" declaring, "Behold, the tabernacle of God is with men, and he will dwell with them, and they shall be his people, and God himself shall be with them, and be their God" (Rev.21:3).

Compare these words with those of our Saviour in John 14. In that passage, He spoke of many dwelling places existing within the Father's house. John's vision develops the picture further, for we discover that the divine purpose is for God to actually dwell *with* His people. The return of the Lord Jesus is for this very purpose – that those who belong to Him might dwell with Him, where He is.

If we look at the description of the city in Revelation 21, it will give us some idea of what the Father's house, within that city, will be like. In his vision John saw "the holy Jerusalem, descending out of heaven from God" (v.10). The city possessed "the glory of God" and shone like a most precious stone. It resembled a jasper stone and was "clear as crystal". Within the wall there were twelve gates, and those gates were guarded by twelve angels. Each gate was associated with one of the tribes of Israel. The city possessed perfect symmetry, with three gates being linked to each point of the compass, while the city's wall had twelve foundations relating to the twelve apostles of the Lamb (v.11—14). The wall was constructed of jasper, and the city itself was made of pure gold which resembled clear glass in its sparkling purity. The wall's foundation was embellished with precious stones, twelve different ones being counted by John (v.18,19). Neither the sun nor the moon was needed to illuminate the city, for it shone with the glory of God and the Lamb (v.23).

What a vision of splendour! If the city displayed such glory, does this not give us some idea of the magnificence of the Father's home within that city?

> *Bright home of our Saviour, what glories await*
> *The spirits that pass through thy bright, pearly gate!*
> *What anthems of rapture, unceasing and high,*
> *Compose the loud chorus that gladdens the sky!*
>
> *The home that our Saviour has gone to prepare —*
> *No heart can conceive of the blessedness there;*
> *Of raptures unending awaiting the just*
> *When pure in His likeness they rise from the dust.*
> *Home! Home! Sweet, sweet home!*
> *Prepare me, dear Saviour, for yonder blest home.*

The truth is that we *do* need preparing for that home. We cannot enter in as we are. How can we be made ready for heaven? One final point needs to be covered as we look at the word H-O-M-E — and that is our *entrance* to it.

The *Entrance* to that Home

Some places have a number of entrances to them. A large house may have a front door, a back door, and a side door. If you visit a stately home you may see a sign saying "Tradesmen's Entrance". Those who are delivering goods or are calling to engage in work on the building will enter by that door; more dignified or important visitors will be expected to enter by another way.

The bungalow where I lived in my childhood had two doors, but the front door was never used. To reach it involved a longer walk from the road where parking was impossible, so it made sense always to use the back door. All callers seemed to know this. The post, the milk, the bread, the newspapers — all were delivered to the back door. If somebody who did not know us called (perhaps canvassing for something or other) and used the front door, we would have to go to the trouble of moving a blind that kept the bright sun out and unlocking the door. My grandparents' house in the same road was just the same. Everybody used the back entrance, but in their case the front door was virtually impossible to open. I think the carpet was wedged too tightly against it!

In John 14 the Lord Jesus had spoken about leaving His disciples and going to the Father's house. They *knew* where He was going, He told them, and they knew the way there (v.4). Thomas remonstrated. "Lord," he said, somewhat plaintively perhaps, "we don't know where You are going, so how can we know the way?" (cf.v.5). To the perplexed disciple, Jesus gave an answer that has become synonymous with true Christianity. "I am the way, the truth, and the life," the Saviour responded. "No man cometh unto the Father, but by me" (v.6).

On a mountain pass (I cannot remember where) at a roadside park were four beautiful stairways, each one facing a different direction. It was possible to climb about fifteen feet up a number of steps on one of the stairways and enjoy a breathtaking view in one direction. Having done this, energetic visitors could then climb one of the other stairways and experience another wonderful view in a *different* direction. Each stairway provided a view of spectacular scenery, but each one only went so far before stopping. It could take you no higher. This illustrates the world's religions very well. It is possible to embrace one religion and find that you have been given an esoteric experience and elevated morally. But notice this: *you are only taken so far*. World religions cannot bring you to the Father — and neither can Christianity if it is taken up as a religion. The Lord Jesus made it abundantly plain that nobody can come "unto the Father, **but by me**" [emphasis added]. Only the Son of God, sent by the Father to save sinners, can bring us *to* the Father.

Elsewhere the Lord Jesus spoke of Himself as *the door*. "By me, if any man enter in, he shall be saved" (Jn.10:9). It is as individuals ("any man") that we come. How can we enter? First, we must repent of our sins. This is not a matter of simply "saying a prayer" but of genuinely being sorry for the ways in which we have offended a holy God. We must turn away from that sin; then we must see what Jesus Christ has done by taking our place upon the cross and bearing our punishment. We must ask Him to save us from our sins and take full control of our lives. There is *no other way*. Nobody can approach God the Father in any other way than through the Son. Have *you* taken that step?

The home we have been thinking about is within a city, and the only ones who enter the city are those who are known to the Lamb of God and whose names are recorded in His book of life (Rev.21:27). At the risk of repeating myself, I emphasize that there is only *one* way to reach the Father's house. The Lord Jesus is that Way.

Homeless

Homelessness is sad to encounter, but how tragic for a soul to be homeless eternally! Nothing can compare with the ruin of being lost from God for ever. But we need not be lost! The Lord Jesus gave up His heavenly home and entered a world where He had no place to lay His head (Lk.9:58). Surely it is touching to think that He left His heavenly home behind in order that He might open it to us. As the Rich One, He deliberately became poor for our sakes so that, through His poverty, we might become rich (2 Cor.8:9). Such was "the grace of our Lord Jesus Christ," and we ought to ponder it well. We did not deserve such a thing, and yet He was prepared to live on earth without a home before dying in our place upon a shameful cross!

If we are true believers, a HOME awaits us in heaven. The Lord Jesus asked His Father that those who had been given to Him should be *with Him* [emphasis added] in the Father's house, where they might view His glory (Jn.17:24). Another lovely children's hymn describes "that beautiful place He has gone to prepare for all who are washed and forgiven". [4] Yes, the Lord Jesus has gone to prepare a beautiful place for us. One day He is coming back for His people so that they might be "at home" with Him for ever.

---

[4] The hymn *I think when I read that sweet story of old* was written by Mrs. Jemima Luke.

Chapter 5

The Paradise of God

Where the saints in glory thronging,
Where they feed on life's blest tree—
There is stilled each earnest longing,
Satisfied our souls shall be.

Safety — where no foe approaches;
Rest — where toil shall be no more;
Joy — whereon no grief encroaches;
Peace — where strife shall all be o'er.

Where deceiver ne'er can enter,
Sin-soiled feet have never trod;
Free — our peaceful feet may venture
In the paradise of God.

Drink of life's perennial river,
Feed on life's perennial food,
Christ, the fruit of life, and giver —
Safe through His redeeming blood.

Object of eternal pleasure,
Perfect in Thy work divine!
Lord of glory! Without measure
Worship, joy and praise are Thine.

J. N. Darby

When He was on earth, the Lord Jesus Christ often spoke about the life to come. In a previous chapter we considered the account recorded in Luke 16 of the rich man and the beggar. (Personally, I do not believe this was simply a "parable" but an actual incident that the Saviour recounted.) Gone from this life, the rich man found himself in a place of torment, while the beggar found himself in a place of bliss. *He* was the one who possessed faith. In John 14 we have the Lord's own words about the Father's house, a place that He has gone to prepare for His blood-bought people. In this chapter we shall consider that place under a different name: *paradise*.

However, before looking at what paradise actually is, I think it is important for us to consider what the Lord Jesus told us about that which lies beyond the grave. There are a few passages of Scripture that ought to be considered.

Matthew 7:13,14 describes two ways that lie before us. There are two destinations that need to be thought about, described as *destruction* and *life*. A wide gate, accommodating people of all kinds, leads to a broad way. We can think of a society where everything is relative and not absolute. All lifestyles, all religions, and all philosophies are accepted, with very few questions being asked. It all sounds rather like the society in which many of us live in twenty-first century Britain. Politicians encourage such things as diversity, openness, equality, and tolerance. But there is one problem — and what a major problem it is! This "broad way" leads to destruction. Alarmingly, "many" are treading that way.

There is another way, however, and it could hardly present more of a contrast. It is a "narrow way" that is entered by a "strait" gate. Clearly it is not a popular way because only a few people are treading it. Courage and determination are needed in order to enter that gate. It will mean standing out from the crowd and being different. But even though few find this way, it is the path that leads to life.

We need to understand that the unpopular path is actually the safe one. If people carry on treading the broad way they will, in the end, reach destruction. Our present position and state certainly affects our future. Only those who have entered through the narrow gate will avoid destruction. The warning from the Lord Jesus Christ is solemn.

Another passage of Scripture should be considered. The words recorded in Matthew 18:8,9 seem to be teaching the need for drastic action. The Lord Jesus warned of being "cast into everlasting fire" and spoke of measures that should be taken to avoid this. A hand, a foot, or an eye could cause the individual offence. If they do, it is better to remove them than face eternal ruin. I do not believe that the

Lord expects us to interpret this on a purely literal basis. There is a *principle* enshrined in this teaching that must be understood. Suppose your hand is being used to engage in some act that is displeasing to God, or your foot takes you to some place where God does not want you to be. Your eye might be focusing on things that are impure, allowing sin to enter into your life. If any of these things are happening, deal with the habit or the action! Break it! If action is not taken, you may find that although the "pleasure" has been retained your soul has been lost. [5] We must be prepared to do what may seem costly and punitive *now* in order to avoid what might happen *later*. Any "loss" in this life is *nothing* compared to eternal loss. In Mark's account, it is stated that the fire "never shall be quenched" (Mk.9:43). The subject is deadly serious!

In Matthew 22 we read the parable of a wedding feast. The king who had invited guests was incredulous to think that so many had refused to come, but new invitations were issued and eventually the hall was filled. When the king came in at the appointed hour, he discovered one man who was not wearing the standard wedding garment but had dressed as he wished. "Friend, how camest thou in hither not having a wedding garment?" he asked (v.12). The man was speechless. The king ordered his servants to bind the man (who was deemed to be an intruder) and "cast him into outer darkness" — the place of "weeping and gnashing of teeth" (v.13).

What a frightful scene this is! Here was a man who thought he knew best and chose to come his own way. So many people do this still. Proud of their achievements, and full of their own merits, they attempt to receive God's blessings by their own means instead of

---

[5] I am not implying that salvation may be lost. It is the *principle* that I am considering here. An unsaved individual who is not prepared to forsake their sin, and repent, will be lost. But a believer should not presume upon the grace of God and treat sin lightly. Scripture clearly teaches that sinful habits should be forsaken.

coming *His* way. They will ultimately discover, to their eternal peril, that they are lost.

At the end of Matthew 25 we have the parable of the sheep and the goats. The parable describes a future time when the Lord Jesus will come in glory and gather people from all the nations to stand before Him for judgment (see v.31,32). Without looking at the parable in detail, simply notice what the Lord pointed out about the "everlasting fire" (v.41). It was originally "prepared for the devil and his angels." God did not purpose that men and women should go there, but those who refuse His gracious offer of salvation and remain in the devil's clutch will accompany him to that place of ruin. Matthew 25:46 clearly identifies two destinies, and both are for ever. It is a case of either "everlasting punishment" or "life eternal". According to His words, not mine, both have no ending.

These verses do not make pleasant reading, and many people are offended to be told of eternal punishment. The truth is not always pleasant, but it needs to be told. Our Lord Jesus Christ is "the way, *the truth*, and the life" (Jn.14:6) [emphasis added]. *He* is the one who spoke these words. They are not to be ignored or airbrushed from existence. If we understand *something* of them, they will help to give us a better appreciation of paradise.

Thoughts about Paradise

I wonder what you think of when somebody mentions paradise. When I first heard of it, I was a young child. In our sitting room were some very unusual curtains (at least, to a small boy they were unusual!) with brightly-coloured birds on them. I must have asked my mother what they were and been told that they were birds of paradise. I recall them having long tails and resembling small peacocks! Outside the sitting room window was our garden. Tall trees grew there, and flowerbeds surrounded the lawn. Birds could frequently be seen in the garden, and on summer evenings a blackbird or a thrush would perch on the roof of the bungalow or in one of the tall trees and sing sweetly. I recall being in that room on a summer evening with the curtains drawn. (Perhaps I had been put in there to sleep rather than in my usual room.) The birds could be heard singing loudly outside as the evening sun shone brightly through the colourful curtains. On the curtains were those unusual birds which I had been told were birds of paradise. I knew that they belonged to faraway places where everything was very different.

Paradise is an oriental word that was first used by the historian Xenophon to describe the parks of Persian kings and nobles. This Persian word passed into Greek as *paradeisos*. It you break up this word it means, literally, "a wall around" and thus refers to a protected walled-garden. The word *paradeisos* is found a number of times in the Septuagint (Greek Old Testament) including Genesis 2:8. In English we read that "the LORD God planted a garden eastward in Eden," but the Septuagint says that He planted a *paradise* there. This is a very interesting reference because it takes us back to before the Fall, to before the time that sin invaded our planet.

On Saturday 13th June, 2015, an elderly friend of my wife and I was taken from us into the presence of the Lord. She had been ill for some weeks, and we knew that the end of her life had been near. Nevertheless my wife, in particular, knew that she would miss her when the Lord called her into His presence.

That same day my wife and I drove to the New Forest and spent an enjoyable time in the open countryside. As we motored back through Mottisfont in the evening, we noticed a lot of cars in the Abbey car park and wondered what was happening. We decided to investigate and soon discovered that it was one of the few evenings in the year when the gardens were open late. People had been enjoying those gardens, but the problem (by the time we arrived) was that most people were leaving! To my wife's great disappointment the last entries to the gardens had been at 7.30 pm, and we were about ten minutes too late. I decided to ask anyway, and the lady at the entrance kindly took pity on us and said, "Go on, but be quick. The gardens will be locked at eight o'clock!"

No second invitation was necessary, and we made tracks to the garden as quickly as we could. We soon reached a beautiful, old, walled rose-garden. The experience of being in it was quite unique. It was not actually one garden, but I think there were three — one leading into another. The soft summer air was filled with the fragrance of hundreds of roses. We listened to the melodious song of birds and heard the humming of numberless bees. It was just so tranquil! We strolled around and lingered within those walls for as long as we could, savouring every moment. We talked of Mary, our departed friend, who had loved her own little garden. "Wouldn't she have enjoyed being here?" we said. But then my mind began to work. What is a "walled garden?" Why, it's paradise! We felt that the Lord was very graciously giving us a little foretaste of God's Paradise to which Mary had gone.

Heaven and earth are not totally unrelated. There are certain similarities between the two. Let me explain what I mean. When Moses was commanded to construct the tabernacle, he was told by God to follow the pattern that he had been shown. What sort of pattern was that? The tabernacle to be constructed was simply a "shadow of heavenly things" (Heb.8:5). Although it was material and tangible, it was really only a *shadow*. A worshipper in Israel of old could *see* the tabernacle and might approach it. When it was assembled and dismantled the Levites could even *touch* the structure. The fact remained, however, that it was just the shadow of something else. The *real* tabernacle existed in heaven and was much better.

We may be surprised to learn that there is an altar in heaven, according to Revelation 16:7. It does seem, from these verses, that the things of God that we are familiar with on earth exist in a far superior form in heaven.

I feel that this rather long introduction has been necessary to prepare the way for our look at paradise. The word is used on three occasions in the New Testament: Luke 23:43, 2 Corinthians 12:4, and Revelation 2:7. We shall take up each of these references in turn.

The Tranquillity of Paradise

And Jesus said unto him, Verily I say unto thee, today shalt thou be with me in paradise.
Luke 23:43

The Lord Jesus had been crucified between two "malefactors" or *evil workers*. As He hung upon the cross He was mocked by the people who stood around and by the religious leaders who sneered, "He saved others; let him save himself, if he be Christ, the chosen of God." The soldiers joined in the taunts as they offered Him vinegar and jeered, "If thou be the king of the Jews, save thyself." An inscription had been placed over His head to identify Him. It said, "This is the King of the Jews." It was written in three languages (Greek, Latin, and Hebrew) so that all who passed by this cosmopolitan place might understand (v.33—38).

The malefactors joined in the abuse, and one of them sneered, "If thou be Christ, save thyself and us." He had no respect for the Lord Jesus and just wanted some means of getting himself away from where he hung. But the other man (who earlier had railed at the Lord Jesus) now disagreed and rebuked his fellow-felon. This was no time to say such things! Their lives were almost over! Surely, he said, it is time for us to *fear* God because we are all condemned. However, there remained an enormous difference. In the case of the two malefactors, their condemnation was just. They were receiving "the due reward of [their] deeds" as they hung there, but "this man" (the

Lord Jesus) had done "nothing amiss" (v.39—41). Perhaps the words he had heard earlier had opened his eyes to recognize the Messiah, for Jesus had cried, "Father, forgive them; for they know not what they do" (v.34). Then, as a broken and contrite man, the malefactor pleaded, "Lord, remember me when thou comest into thy kingdom" (v.42). Here is the clearest proof that he knew he was in the company of One who was different from any other.

The answer to his request was more than he could ever have expected. There was no need to wait for a coming kingdom! "*Today*," said Jesus, [emphasis added] "shalt thou be with me in paradise" (v.43). What a wonderful promise! The man was suffering intensely. Pain racked his body as he hung suspended above the earth under the blazing sun. The heat, the noise, the words of mockery, the hatred, the blasphemy ... all would soon be over! It was as though the Lord Jesus was saying to him, "I will take you out of here to be with Me. I will take you into the bliss and peace of paradise today!"

What a message of hope this is for those who have none! All who belong to the Lord Jesus Christ can share this wondrous prospect. One day He will take us away from all our pain and suffering and from the sin, unrest, and blasphemy that surround us daily. He will take us to a place of safety and tranquillity — behind those secure walls. We shall enter into the fulness of God's peace which surpasses our understanding (cf. Phil.4:7). What an incomparable future awaits the child of God!

The Transcendence of Paradise

How that he was caught up into paradise ...
2 Corinthians 12:4

Believers in the church at Corinth were boasting of their gifts and experiences, and the apostle Paul felt compelled to join them (2 Cor.11:18) although he did not really want to do so (12:11a)! He writes about "a man in Christ" whom he knew, though clearly the reference is to himself. Paul could have presented his experience with the authority of an apostle, but he felt it would be more effective to mask himself — hence the expression "a man in Christ".

The man Paul describes had had a remarkable experience. Some fourteen years earlier he had been "caught up to the third heaven" (v.2). This indicates that there must be a first and a second heaven. We can consider the first heaven to be the atmospheric heavens, while the second heaven refers to the stellar heavens which lie beyond. The third heaven brings us to the location of God's throne. The man may have been caught up bodily into God's presence, or it may have been an experience in which his spirit was briefly removed from his body and transported there. If Paul did not know which it was, it is pointless for us to speculate!

Caught up into paradise, this man "heard unspeakable words, which it is not lawful for a man to utter" (v.4). Why could those words not be uttered? How we wish they *had* been recorded for us! What prevented Paul from reporting them? First, those words may have been beyond our understanding. The prohibition may have been because our finite minds would have been unable to grasp their meaning. A second reason is that those words may have been too holy. They had been uttered in a realm where sin was totally absent and may have been too sacred to bring before us. God, in His wisdom, has seen fit to withhold their meaning from us.

To prevent Paul boasting of his remarkable experience, "a thorn in the flesh, the messenger of Satan" was sent to "buffet" him (v.7). Again, we would love to know exactly what Paul meant but are not told in as many words — though some scholars think they have discovered it! There is good reason why we are not told as we can effectively apply the trial to ourselves. Although Paul's "thorn in the flesh" was not removed, he *did* discover an abounding supply of grace from God to sustain him in it (v.9).

Our loving Father knows what is best for us too, and He may allow some kind of "thorn in the flesh" to trouble us in order that we do not become puffed up with pride. Although that "thorn" may be difficult to bear, His grace is "sufficient" for the trial and is freely available, on request, to help us each day. But as we receive that grace we can also look forward to paradise — the place that transcends any earthly "paradise" that may provide a foretaste of heaven. One day all believers will be "caught up" like Paul, at the coming of the Lord. When that happens and we enter paradise, *then* we will understand the things that Paul was not allowed to share with us — wonderful though they were!

The Transplantation of Paradise

To him that overcometh will I give to eat of the tree of life, which is in the midst of the paradise of God.
Revelation 2:7

People in the church at Ephesus had lost their first love for the Lord (v.4). At one time they had been overjoyed with Him; He mattered more than anything else. Sadly, that had changed. Routine had crept in, and many had become complacent and lethargic, taking Him for granted. It was time to act! They needed to "remember" what they were at one time and repent of their true condition. It was essential to return to the Lord and to being the kind of people they were previously (v.5). If anyone heeded the warning, and overcame the spirit of lethargy, a promise was given. Such a person would be permitted to "eat of the tree of life, which is in the midst of the paradise of God."

This reference to the tree of life takes us back in thought to the opening chapters of the Bible. Genesis 2:9 describes "the tree of life" which was located "in the midst of the garden". The same tree is mentioned again in the next chapter. After his disobedience, Adam was banished from Eden in case he might "put forth his hand, and take also of the tree of life, and eat, and live for ever" (Gen.3:22). He had already disobeyed his Creator by reaching out and taking of the tree of the knowledge of good and evil. It would have been tragic if he had taken of the tree of life *also* — for having done so in a fallen condition, he would have been made to live for ever in his misery! For this reason, our first parents were banished from that beautiful paradise in Eden.

In Revelation 2 we discover the tree of life again. This time it is to be found in another garden. The tree which had once grown in Eden is now found flourishing "in the midst of the paradise of God" (v.7). The connection is unavoidable. In Eden, the tree of life was "in the midst of the garden"; here in paradise it again occupies a central position. The difference, however, is that it is no longer a forbidden tree. The "overcomer" is invited to draw near and partake of its fruit — which is not seasonal like so many of our earthly fruits. The tree is nourished by the river of life and yields "twelve manner of fruits" corresponding to the months of the year (Rev.22:2). There is a boundless supply! Endless life is thus nourished in paradise. We discover the *transplantation* of the tree that offers life in all its fulness.

Springtime

Spring is such a beautiful time of the year. The newly-opened leaves are so bright and fresh and present such a contrast with the bleak winter that has passed. April and May are months when many gardens are filled with brightly-coloured flowers. Daffodils are followed by crocuses and tulips. Rhododendrons and azaleas flourish out in the country on appropriate hillsides, and many nature-lovers flock to famous gardens where they can stroll at leisure and enjoy the dazzling display of cultivated rhododendrons and azaleas.

The colours are breath-taking, but the effects of sin are always near. You do not have to look very far before you see weeds, nettles, thorns, and brambles — all being products of the Fall.

A home on earth often has a garden that the occupants can enjoy. Heaven is very similar. If there is such a place as the Father's house, there is also paradise! Paradise is the "walled-garden" that belongs to the heavenly Home. If we enjoy the beauties of this earth, how much better that garden will be! [6]

It is not *good* people who look forward to its tranquility but repentant and forgiven people, those like the dying thief. We can enjoy foretastes of paradise now, but paradise transcends all that we can know down here. Life is found in Christ alone and will continue *with* Him, in paradise, for ever.

---

[6] In his hymn *There is a land of pure delight* (quoted in Chapter 2) Isaac Watts referred to the "never-withering flowers" found there.

Chapter 6

<u>That Beautiful Shore</u>

There's a land that is fairer than day,
And by faith we can see it afar,
For the Father waits over the way,
To prepare us a dwelling-place there.

In the sweet ... by-and-by
We shall meet on that beautiful shore,
In the sweet ... by-and-by
We shall meet on that beautiful shore.

We shall sing on that beautiful shore
The melodious songs of the blest,
And our spirits shall sorrow no more —
Not a sigh for the blessing of rest.

To our bountiful Father above
We will offer the tribute of praise,
For the glorious gift of His love,
And the blessings that hallow our days.

Sanford F. Bennett

The internet has become a mine of information and enables people with access to it to make their purchases without having to visit shops. Many businesses have been "feeling the pinch" with this new-style consumer spending. Travel agents have not been immune from the internet's competition as holiday-makers can book their excursions online without having to spend time discussing their preferences with someone at a desk. Eventually the printed glossy holiday brochures with which we are so familiar may become a thing of the past. However, that point has not yet been reached — and it is still possible to walk into a travel agency and be confronted with an array of glossy brochures.

Holiday brochures are produced with one intention in mind. The company selling the holiday will promote a destination in such a way as to arouse interest. The pictures used and the description of the resort combine to captivate the prospective tourist so that, after finding out about the destination, the person will say, "I really want to go there!" It would be a very unusual kind of person who would book a holiday without knowing anything about the destination. It is important to find out what the weather will be like and what you will be able to see and do. Indeed, if somebody wants to derive enjoyment from visiting a very different place they will find out all that they can about the place before setting off.

If a little research is done before a holiday which may last a week or two, how much more important it is to find out about another country in which you might live! If you are going to emigrate, you will not do so without knowing about the land to which you will move. How absurd it would be to uproot from familiar surroundings and emigrate to a country about which you knew absolutely nothing!

By the same token, if we are going to heaven when our life on earth is over, should we not find out *now* as much as we can about the place where we shall live eternally?

One Brochure

Only one book can help us in our search to find out what that "destination" will be like, and that book is the Bible. But we soon discover we are told very little about heaven! The reason for this lack of detail is probably because we could not fully understand what we were told anyway. Heaven is totally different from any earthly place. The main reason for this is that *sin* is absent from heaven.

The earlier chapters in this book have explained that heaven can be compared to a *country* and a *city*. Abraham, you may recall, desired "a better country" (Heb.11:16) and "a city … whose builder and maker is God" (Heb.11:10). But heaven is also presented as a *home*. The Lord Jesus spoke of His Father's "house" (Jn.14:2). Another figure used to help us understand heaven is a *garden*. The word *paradise* is used three times in the New Testament and describes a perfect, secure environment away from all danger and harm. These concepts help us to understand a little about what will be the saints' eternal home. We can be absolutely sure that the best we enjoy down here will not compare with what God has prepared for us up there — though on earth God may be pleased to give us a little foretaste of heaven.

From these different figures used we learn a little bit about heaven, but what can be said about *reaching* heaven? How can we understand the journey which must be taken, or the transition from one realm to another? Death is the means that God currently uses to bring His people there, and this explains the Scripture that "precious in the sight of the LORD is the death of his saints" (Ps.116:15). But death is not something mortals relish or enjoy discussing!

A few years ago, when American-style "pre-paid funerals" were launched in Britain, an advert was placed on T.V. One marketing director recommended purchasing a funeral in advance. Such a step would, in his words, "take the sting out of death" for people could make the purchase, forget about dying, and get on with their living. We all know that it is not cheap to die! Any help, therefore, with escalating funeral costs is bound to be good. However, we must not imagine that once the funeral has been paid for in advance we can forget about death and get on with living! Death has a sting — and that sting is not removed by arranging a pre-paid funeral package! According to the Bible, death has lost its sting and the grave its victory because of what has been won by our Lord Jesus Christ (1 Cor.15:55;57)! By His own death and resurrection, He has defeated this fearsome enemy. Death's sting has been removed for the believer in Christ, because if we die we shall be raised from the grave at His return. Even now we can know something of being delivered from that sting.

There are two further figures that can help us understand death. Both concepts are simple and are used in the New Testament. One is the figure of *sleeping*; the other is the figure of *sailing*. We are familiar with both ideas. Sleeping is something we do (or want to do!) each night. Sailing, too, is not a difficult idea to grasp. We understand what it means to board a ship and to set sail for another port. In this chapter we shall explore both ideas.

The Figure of Sleeping

The first thing to consider is the *painlessness* of sleep. Surely no lengthy explanation of this fact is necessary! If sleeping was painful we would not allow ourselves to fall asleep. The normal sleeping person would be seen writhing in agony if sleep was painful — but that is not the case. Picture a little child who has been busily playing out of doors and has worn himself out. After coming inside, it may not be long before that child is asleep. The child is willing and ready to sleep because he has no fears. Neither is there any sign of pain when we look at the sleeping child. No-one thinks of rushing to the side of the child in order to rouse him from his slumbers, exclaiming as they do, "Poor child! We can't let him lie there sleeping. He must be in such pain! We must rouse him at once to stop him suffering any more!" Anyone doing such a thing would be mad! The child is tired from his activity and is being restored physically by sleep. Rest is beneficial.

Consider the accounts in the gospels of those who died. Very often the Lord Jesus referred to death as sleep. Although the twelve-year-old daughter of Jairus had died, Jesus called it being asleep. Those present in the house laughed Him to scorn but soon discovered that death, to Him, was of no more consequence than sleep. He simply took the young girl by the hand and raised her to life and health again (Mt.9:24,25). In His presence death need not be feared!

Lazarus had been a very sick man. When the Lord Jesus took His disciples to Bethany where Lazarus was, He explained that the purpose of the visit was to arouse Lazarus from his sleep. The

70

disciples misunderstood and could only think of sleep in physical terms. If Lazarus was asleep, it was a hopeful sign, they thought! Peaceful sleep could help to restore the sick man. Jesus, however, was referring to *death* as He spoke of Lazarus sleeping (Jn.11:11—13). He spoke in this way to show that there is nothing to fear.

If we are called upon to die, the state of death is painless. *Before* death there can certainly be pain. The person about to die may be restless and may be tossing in agony upon their bed, but death itself will bring relief to the pain-racked body. Just as the person who is physically asleep is not experiencing pain, the believer who has died has been freed from pain. The body you look at is experiencing *no more pain*. All the suffering of this life is over! So for the saved individual, passing from this life is just like falling asleep. *Painlessness* is a term that describes the experience.

A second idea to grasp as we think of sleep, or death for the believer, is its *pleasantness*. We know that sleep is pleasant, because through it we escape from the ongoing problems of life. The death of the martyr, Stephen, illustrates this truth. He had been accused of speaking "blasphemous words against this holy place [the temple], and the law" and was brought before the Sanhedrin (Acts 6:13). As he concluded his defence, he charged his bigoted listeners with rank hypocrisy. They were part of a nation that had rejected their Messiah! Wanting to hear no more of such things, his infuriated accusers "were cut to the heart, and they gnashed on him with their teeth" (Acts 7:54). Filled with the Holy Spirit, Stephen "looked up steadfastly into heaven, and saw the glory of God, and Jesus standing on the right hand of God" (Acts 7:55).

What a vision that was! Stephen could not keep it to himself but told his listeners in tones of triumph, "Behold, I see the heavens opened, and the Son of man standing on the right hand of God" (Acts 7:56). That was enough! They cried out in anger to drown Stephen's voice and rushed upon him in fury. Dragging him bodily from the city, they began to pelt the godly man with stones. His accusers hastily discarded any long robes that interfered with their heinous deed and cast them at the feet of a young man named Saul. As they stoned Stephen, he called out to God with the words, "Lord Jesus, receive my spirit". He then knelt down and, with a loud voice, prayed in very similar fashion to his Saviour at the cross: "Lord, lay not this sin to their charge". Having prayed for his enemies, and having committed his soul to his Saviour, Stephen then "fell asleep" (Acts 7:57—60).

Think of that! Here was a man who had been stoned to death and had experienced vitriolic hatred, yet he could simply fall asleep! Why can such an experience be considered *pleasant*? The answer is that Stephen had seen the Lord Jesus in glory and had appealed to Him to receive his spirit. He was at peace as he went to meet his Saviour.

Hebrews 4:9 speaks of a coming "rest" for the people of God. Night by night as we lie down to sleep, we enter into a *physical* state of rest. But there is also a *spiritual* state of rest into which we can enter. Rest is not something that we fear! As Stephen "fell asleep" he entered into rest. His sufferings on earth were over. The body of a departed person lies still and resembles the body of someone who is sleeping. The believer who "falls asleep" in Jesus enters into rest immediately. In the words of Scripture, they are "absent from the body ... present with the Lord" (2 Cor.5:8).

The Figure of Sailing

The other figure that is used to describe the believer's transition from earth to heaven which we shall look at in this chapter is *sailing*. In Hebrews 6:20 the Greek word *prodromos* (translated "forerunner") is used to describe Jesus as One who has gone in advance of us, or before us. We need to understand what happened many years ago in the days of sailing ships to appreciate this verse. During a storm, when it was dangerous for a ship to enter the port, a small boat would carry the ship's anchor into the harbour. The anchor would be safely secured within the harbour, and when it was safe the ship would sail in to its anchorage. All the time it was secured to its anchor by a strong cable.

The figure is very descriptive. God, we are told, cannot lie. He offers us "strong consolation" through "the hope [that is] set before us." Our hope is described as "an anchor of the soul, both sure and steadfast" and is "within the veil". The veil speaks of the holy presence of God where the Lord Jesus (our "forerunner") has entered. He is there as our Great High Priest and represents us before God.

"Within the veil" corresponds to the harbour. After His earthly ministry was over, the Lord Jesus was "carried up into heaven" (Lk.24:51). He has carried our hope into heaven *with* Him. That hope is as firm as an anchor for the soul and is "sure and steadfast". Applying the imagery used, *we* are the storm-tossed ship outside the harbour, connected by a strong cable to the anchor that has been carried in to the harbour. Our Great High Priest does not forget us! One day we, too, shall enter the heavenly harbour where our Forerunner has gone. A further feature from this imagery is not to be missed. The dinghy that enters the harbour first is small compared to the ship that remains outside. Our Lord Jesus has graciously gone before us, and in His great humility we are precious to Him. He considers it important to bring us into the safety of the harbour. The true believer can confidently sing, "I've anchored in Jesus," and can look forward to the time when we all shall meet Him "within the veil".

Hebrews 6:20 reminds us that our *Forerunner* has entered heaven "for us". This means *we* shall follow Him there one day. Before concluding this chapter, we shall consider one of the many *followers* of the Lord Jesus — a man who teaches us some important truths. In

Acts 7:58 we have already met this "young man" whose name was Saul. He was one who would never forget witnessing the martyrdom of Stephen. In due time he was converted and became one of Christ's committed followers. As Paul the apostle, he develops this theme of sailing and uses the expression in his epistles.

In Philippians 1:23 Paul explained a conflict that he was experiencing. He was torn between two strong desires and found it difficult to know which to choose. On the one hand he very much wanted to see his friends at Philippi again and share with them things that would bring encouragement. There was, however, a stronger desire. This was "to depart and to be with Christ" and this, Paul knew, would be "far better". The word translated as *depart* means to unloose, or to set sail. Paul pictured himself sailing from his restricted life here into the freedom of eternity.

The same expression is used in 2 Timothy 4:6. In his final preserved letter Paul declares that he is ready to be poured out in death. Nothing is held back. "The time of my departure is at hand," he says. Scholars of the Greek language tell us that rich imagery can be found here. An army or a traveller breaking camp would speak of *departing* in this way. Like them, Paul was about to take out the tent pegs (figuratively speaking) and begin his march. A ploughman, at the end of the day, would unyoke his weary horses. They had toiled long and hard in the fields, but now they were to *depart* from their bondage and experience freedom and rest in the stable. Similarly, Paul's labours were over. He was about to enter into his eternal rest. The expression was also used to describe a philosopher who had teased his brain over a problem that he was determined to solve. When the solution was discovered, it meant his *departure* from what had occupied him for so long. Finally, the term described the ship that was about to be loosed from its moorings and set sail.

Paul's ship was about to leave the harbour. His earthly race had been run. He had "fought a good fight" (meaning he had agonized in the athletic contest) and had finished his course. Like the athlete participating in a relay race, he had completed his section. He had also "kept the faith" by maintaining the purity of the doctrines which had been entrusted to him. He could look forward to the "crown of righteousness" that was reserved for him and would be placed upon his head by his righteous Lord in a coming day. But the reward would not be for him alone. All whose eyes by faith are fixed upon the Lord Jesus and who look forward to His promised return will receive that same crown (2 Tim.4:7,8).

What a moment it will be when all the followers of Jesus reach the safety of the heavenly harbour! It has often been asked whether we will recognize one another when we reach our home in heaven. Opinions differ, but I believe that we shall. My belief is based upon the transfiguration scene, described in Matthew 17 (as well as in Mark and Luke). On the mountain-top Peter was able to recognize Moses and Elijah although he had never met them before. Moses and Elijah were not contemporaries. Moses had lived hundreds of years before Elijah and had, at the end of his life, been buried in a secret location. Elijah, on the other hand, had never died but had been transported miraculously to glory by a whirlwind. Yet both of them were united in a scene that Peter could enjoy, along with James and John. So thrilled was Peter with the experience that he wanted it to continue!

We may have lived at different periods of time, centuries apart. Yet all the followers of Jesus will be united in the Lord's presence, and when we see Him in His glory we shall not have lost our individual identity. The *Forerunner* has entered the heavenly harbour, and all of His *followers* will reach it too — in His own good time.

"We shall meet on that beautiful shore ... "

The words of Sanford F. Bennett assure us that those who love the

LIFE BEYOND THE SUNSET

Lord Jesus and belong to Him will meet again "on that beautiful shore". By faith we look on and up to the "land that is fairer than day" and to the home that awaits us in heaven. Paul longed to be there! Although he loved the people of God and valued their fellowship, he longed for the time when he would enjoy the "far better" experience of being "with Christ" (Phil.1:23). He could tell Timothy of his readiness to depart from the earthly harbour and set sail for the shores of eternity. Very soon the ropes that held him to his earthly moorings would be untied, and he would journey on.

Sometimes a Christian knows that the call is "near" and the time of their departure is "at hand" (2 Tim.4:6) — but are *we* ready? Have we placed our trust in the finished work of Christ at the cross? Do we know Him as Saviour? Have our sins been forgiven? Do we have peace with God through the Lord Jesus Christ? It is so important to be *ready* for our departure.

Ocean crossings can be very slow. It may take a number of days to cross one of the oceans of this world, and ships may be at sea for a few weeks. Records have been made and broken as one ship makes an ocean crossing more quickly than a predecessor — but how long will the crossing into eternity take? Will it be a matter of days, weeks, or months? The answer is that it will be instantaneous! The passing from time into eternity will have happened before we know it! Fanny Crosby wrote:

Some day the silver cord will break,
And I no more as now shall sing;
But, oh, the joy when I shall wake
Within the palace of the King!
And I shall see Him face to face,
And tell the story — saved by grace!

Passing from this world, as we have seen, is very much like going to sleep and waking up again. We shall awake "within the palace of the

76

King!" We shall see Him and shall praise Him for ever for His grace. The experience need not fill us with dread or terror. There is nothing to fear! Because the *Forerunner* has entered the safety of the heavenly harbour, it is guaranteed that all His *followers* will reach it too. These twin ideas of sleeping and sailing can help us understand a little more clearly what it means to cross to the shores of eternity.

Chapter 7

I shall know Him

When my life-work is ended, and I cross the swelling tide,
When the bright and glorious morning I shall see;
I shall know my Redeemer when I reach the other side,
And His smile will be the first to welcome me.
I shall know ... Him, I shall know Him,
When redeemed by His side I shall stand;
I shall know ... Him, I shall know Him
By the print of the nails in His hand.

Oh, the soul-thrilling rapture when I view His blessèd face,
And the lustre of His kindly beaming eye;
How my full heart will praise Him for the mercy, love, and grace,
That prepare for me a mansion in the sky.

Oh, the dear ones in glory, how they beckon me to come,
And our parting at the river I recall;
To the sweet vales of Eden they will sing my welcome home:
But I long to meet my Saviour first of all.

Through the gates of the city, in a robe of spotless white,
He will lead me where no tears will ever fall;
In the glad song of ages I shall mingle with delight:
But I long to meet my Saviour first of all.

Fanny J. Crosby

Some of our experiences in life can remain clearly imprinted upon the mind even though they took place a long time ago. I recall an occasion in 2007 when I was in the West Sussex town of Bognor Regis and was trying to locate a nursing home where someone I knew was living. The initial directions I had been given had proved unhelpful, so I stopped my car outside another nursing home and approached a carer who was pushing someone in a wheelchair. I asked her if she knew the place I was trying to find. She was from another country and could not understand my request very well, so she pointed me to a decorator who was painting the outside of the building. He had not heard of the place I was searching for — and neither had the colleague with whom he was working.

At that moment, the manager of the nursing home appeared and proved to be a more useful source of information. He knew of the place I wanted to find but advised me that my search would be anything but easy. The directions were complicated, but he *did* offer a few helpful landmarks that I ought to look out for on the way — one of which was an inn called "The Lamb". Thanking him for his help, I climbed into my car to continue the search. As I set off I had a number of landmarks in my mind to help me, but I knew that the nursing home was near to an inn. Without knowing it, the man had actually given me an ideal gospel illustration. "You've got to find the Lamb" is, in fact, very good biblical advice!

I found one inn and then another, but not "the Lamb". Then I discovered a *third* inn, but it was called "The Lion". Had the man made a mistake, I wondered. Both words begin with the same letter, so did he really intend that I should be looking out for "The Lion" rather than "The Lamb"? After a little more searching I *did* find "The Lamb" — and much later I also found the nursing home that I was looking for because it had moved to new premises. Before finding it I had to ask more members of the public — including someone who was quenching his thirst in "The Lamb"!

Two words were connected in my mind that day, but a lion and a lamb are very different creatures. You could hardly mistake one for the other! Really, the two animals are opposites. There is, however, a very interesting Bible passage that connects them.

"And one of the elders saith unto me, Weep not: behold, the Lion of the tribe of Judah, the Root of David, hath prevailed to open the book, and to loose the seven seals thereof. And I beheld, and, lo, in the midst of the throne and of the four beasts, and in the midst of the elders, stood a Lamb as it had been slain" (Rev.5:5,6a).

In this fascinating chapter, John had a vision of the throne of God. Seated upon it was the Almighty, and in His hand was a sealed book. A mighty angel had cried and asked who was worthy to break the seals of this book and reveal its contents, but nobody anywhere in the universe responded to the call. The event distressed John, and he "wept much" because no worthy individual could be found. (This is the only record of weeping in heaven.) An elder approached John and gently told him not to weep because "the Lion of the tribe of Judah" was there. He met all the requirements and was worthy to break the seals of the scroll. John turned to look at the Lion but could not see it anywhere. Instead, he saw "A Lamb as it had been slain" in the very centre of the throne (v.1—6). Had John made a mistake? How could he confuse a lion with a lamb? The answer is that the Lion and the Lamb both depict the same Person.

In the beautiful hymn printed at the beginning of this chapter, the blind author, Fanny Crosby, wrote, "I shall know Him ... by the print of the nails in His hand." She was convinced that with restored vision she would recognize her Saviour in heaven, and she would know Him by the wounds in His body.

In the previous chapter we considered the Transfiguration of our Lord. Centuries after they had left this earth, Moses and Elijah were both recognized by Peter — although he had never met either of them before. This incident convinces me that believers *will* recognize one another in heaven. But after the scene of glory faded from Peter's view, "Jesus was found alone" (Lk.9:36), and the disciples "saw no man, save Jesus only" (Mt.17:8). In His glory, He outshone the rest. When Stephen was given a vision of the opened heavens, he saw the Lord Jesus at God's right hand (Acts 7:56). I am sure we *shall* know one another in glory, but I am even more certain that we

81

shall know our Lord Jesus Christ.

In this chapter we are going to consider John's two visions of the Lion and of the Lamb. We shall begin by focusing upon the latter.

The Vision of the Lamb

And I beheld, and, lo, in the midst of the throne ... stood a Lamb as it had been slain ...
Revelation 5:6

The first thing we notice about the Lamb whom John saw is that it appeared to be *slain.* "In the midst of the throne ... stood a Lamb as it had been slain" (v.6). Translators note that the Greek word used here is a diminutive term and generally identifies *a little lamb*, rather like a pet. The Lamb in John's vision was therefore young. Does it not remind us of Israel's Passover? The Lord had instructed His people of old to take a lamb "without blemish, a male of the first year" (Ex.12:5). But the lamb chosen by each Israelite family in Egypt had to die. The Passover pointed forward to the coming of the Lamb of God who would die in the place of lost and guilty sinners.

The theme of the slain Lamb can be traced through the Old Testament. Isaiah wrote of the coming Messiah who would be "brought as a lamb to the slaughter, and as a sheep before her shearers [be] dumb" (Is.53:7). His prophecy was remarkably fulfilled centuries later in Gethsemane when an armed mob entered the garden in order to apprehend the Lord Jesus. The Saviour allowed them to take Him and lead Him away to the house of the high priest (Lk.22:54). No word was uttered in protest by the Saviour. After the indignity of His trial and the cruel treatment meted out by the Roman soldiers, Pilate delivered the Lord Jesus to be crucified — "and they took Jesus, and led him away" (Jn.19:16). Again, no resistance was offered as the Lamb of God silently submitted to the wicked hands of those who had placed a rugged cross upon His back.

He had come into the world for this very purpose. Upon the shameful cross He bore our sins in His own body as He died for us (1 Pet.2:24). Truly, "he was wounded for our transgressions, he was bruised for our iniquities: the chastisement of our peace was upon him; and with his stripes we are healed" (Is.53:5). The One who was meekly led to the slaughter, willingly died in our place. The Lamb John saw in his vision had been *slain*.

However, something quite unusual was noticed by John. The words "in the midst of the throne ... stood a Lamb as it had been slain" (v.6) indicate that the slain Lamb was now *standing*. Normally a creature that has been slain is found lying prone upon the ground — but not here. What can account for the fact that the Lamb was *standing* before John? We need to go back to the gospel written by him. In it, John describes what took place when Jesus was crucified. In order to hasten the victims' deaths, the soldiers were instructed by Pilate to break their legs. They came to the first man crucified, found that life was still in him, and broke his legs. By-passing the centre cross, they then went to the other malefactor and broke his legs too. Finally they came to Jesus, but when they saw that He was dead already they did not break His legs (John 19:32,33). The Lamb of God perfectly fulfilled the requirements of the Passover lamb, for not a bone was to be broken (Ex.12:46).

The gospel records describe the burial of the Lord Jesus (which was undertaken by Joseph of Arimathaea and Nicodemus) and the visit made to the tomb by Mary Magdalene on the first day of the week. Peter and John, mystified by the empty tomb, had returned to their homes while Mary lingered in the garden. As she stood outside, she became conscious of the fact that she was not alone. "She turned herself back, and saw Jesus standing, and knew not that it was Jesus" (Jn.20:14). One can hardly blame her for this. The last time she had seen Him was when He was hanging upon the cross, His hands and feet pierced by cruel nails. But notice that now He is *standing* in the garden. Why can He stand? The answer is thrilling to grasp: He stands because His legs were never broken! Indeed, on the evening of that same day the Lord Jesus entered the room where His disciples were met together and *stood* among them (Lk.24:36).

How appropriate, then, that in his vision John should observe a Lamb *standing* before him (Rev.5:6). Later, in Revelation 14:1, the same Lamb is seen standing upon Mount Zion with 144,000 of His followers. Thinking of His triumph, Horatius Bonar wrote:

> *Rejoice and be glad! For the Lamb that was slain*
> *O'er death is triumphant, and liveth again.* [7]

The slain Lamb is now standing because He has triumphed over death.

But something else must be observed in this vision. The Lamb John can see is a *significant* Lamb because He stands in a central place. "And I beheld, and, lo, *in the midst* of the throne and of the four beasts, and *in the midst* of the elders, stood a Lamb as it had been slain" (Rev.5:6: emphasis added). How often in His earthly ministry the Lord Jesus was seen to be "in the midst" of people! We find Him in that position as a boy of twelve in the temple when He was seen "in the midst" of the rabbinic teachers (Lk.2:46). After His resurrection we discover Him in that same position. John describes the entrance of the Lord Jesus into the room where His disciples had assembled. Without anyone needing to open the doors, Jesus appeared and "stood in the midst" — not at the back, nor in a corner, but right in the centre. We can understand how the disciples were "glad" to see the Lord (Jn.20:19,20)! A week later He occupied the same position ("in the midst") when the disciples met once more but this time with Thomas present (Jn.20:26). God's purpose is that His Son should occupy the central place.

---

[7] From Horatius Bonar's hymn "Rejoice and be glad! The Redeemer has come."

However, we might wonder why His position is one of standing. After returning to heaven He certainly *did* sit down upon His Father's throne (Rev.3:21). Another verse confirms that after enduring the cross and despising the shame the Lord Jesus sat down at the right hand of the throne of God (Heb.12:2). This fact cannot be disputed. But here in Revelation 5:6 He is seen in a standing position because He is about to step forward and take the book from the One seated upon the throne (Rev.5:7). Psalm 110:1 is Messianic (i.e. a psalm speaking of Christ) and records the words of the Father to the Son: "Sit thou at my right hand, until I make thine enemies thy footstool". His being seated is only for a time; it is only *until* His enemies will be brought under His feet. He now stands ready to deal with those enemies.

What a wonderful vision of the Lamb of God standing in heaven's glory! But John had not been told that the *Lamb* had prevailed; his attention had been directed to the *Lion* of the tribe of Judah. We must now consider this second vision.

The Vision of the Lion

Behold, the Lion of the tribe of Judah, the Root of David, hath prevailed to open the book ...
Revelation 5:5

In this verse the *genealogy* of the Lion is disclosed. He belongs to "the tribe of Judah" which was the kingly tribe. As his twelve sons gathered around his deathbed, Jacob prophesied concerning the future of each tribe. Judah was likened to a lion, and we learn that "the sceptre [would] not depart from Judah ... until Shiloh come" (Gen.49:9,10). Shiloh is a somewhat obscure word and is translated in various ways, but there appears to be a Messianic significance in the expression, and the thought of people being gathered to Him seems to confirm this. Certainly the future kings of Israel were to arise from Judah's tribe.

We know, from the Old Testament, that Israel's first king was from the tribe of Benjamin. Although Saul's physique was impressive, he did not possess the hallmarks of a true man of God. As Paul pointed out in Acts 13:21,22, David was the man chosen by God to reign over His people and to begin the line of kings from which the Lord Jesus descended. The angelic announcement at His birth confirmed that Bethlehem was indeed "the city of David" (Lk.2:11).

However, although He *was* a descendant of both Judah and David, the message spoken to John declared that the Lion was the *Root* of David. Israel's first king in the royal line of Judah (David) was indeed promised a significant "Son" who would be greater than Solomon. But a "root" precedes any "fruit" that may be produced. (A rhubarb root can be planted in the soil and, in time, may yield stalks that can be picked — but the root is there before anything it produces.) The expression "the Root of David" therefore indicates that Christ existed *before* David and actually gave David his origin. Being "of the tribe of Judah" indicates His humanity, while the term "the Root of David" reveals His deity. Both are seen together in Revelation 22:16 where the Lord Jesus speaks of Himself as "the root and the offspring of David" as well as "the bright and morning star".

But the Lion has achieved a great *gain*: He has "prevailed" (or overcome). If John had heard that the *Lamb* had overcome, it might not have sounded right. A lamb is a meek and docile creature, whereas the lion is kingly and majestic. It is appropriate to think of the *Lion* overcoming. John had wept to think that nobody was worthy to open the book (v.4); but someone *was* (v.5)! How had He "prevailed"?

Hebrews 2:14,15 explains to us what happened. As human beings possessing "flesh and blood", we were "subject to bondage" throughout life because of the persistent "fear of death" which exerted a relentless control over us. We needed to be delivered. How could this be achieved? The Lord Jesus Christ became a man, like us. He took "flesh and blood" upon Himself and accepted our humanity, though He was not defiled by a sinful nature. Willingly He subjected Himself to death in order to defeat Satan who held the power of death and to deliver us from his clutches. He did something that no human being has ever been able to do by dismissing His spirit, and then He arose triumphant from death because He had the authority to take up His life again. Through His death and resurrection believers are now delivered from that bondage associated with the fear of death. He has won a great victory! In order to do this, the Lion became the Lamb so that He might experience death. But He has prevailed!

Glory is associated with the Lion of the tribe of Judah in Revelation 5. His *worth* is proclaimed, for He is worthy to break the seals of the closed book and read its content. What is the book? Although various suggestions have been made (some nothing more than mere conjecture) we actually are not told what it contains. There are certainly seven seals of judgment that are opened in the following chapters of Revelation. God has His "books" recording the deeds that men have done, and the Lamb possesses His own "book of life" (Rev.21:27). We do not need to settle the question in order to appreciate the scene before us. What we *do* know is that there are insurmountable problems upon earth that man, by his wisdom, is utterly unable to solve. How we need someone who can deal with injustice, reconcile differences, and restore peace between nations. No answer can be found away from the throne of God.

"And he came and took the book out of the right hand of him that sat upon the throne" (v.7). This verse always makes me think of the F. A. Cup Final which is generally held at Wembley Stadium in London each May. At the end of the match, the captain of the winning team leads his colleagues up the steps from the pitch to receive the trophy from a dignitary. As the trophy is triumphantly held aloft, a roar breaks forth from the assembled supporters. It is a moment of victory. Grown men in the winning team often have tears in their eyes as they are overcome by the emotion of the occasion. This match has been the culmination of a victory trail going back over a number of months. The effort put in has been immense, but the hardship experienced and the injuries sustained along the way can now all be forgotten in the elation of this moment!

The rejoicing in heaven will make any such earthly triumph pale into insignificance. A new song of worship bursts forth in praise of the Lamb who was slain to redeem His people. He is worthy to take the book and to open its seals! People from every kindred, tribe, and nation have been brought to God by His sacrifice at the cross (v.9,10). All heaven proclaims, "Worthy is the Lamb that was slain to receive power, and riches, and wisdom, and strength, and honour, and glory, and blessing" (v.12). Around the throne of God are more beings than John can number joining in the great song of praise (v.11).

The Lion is the Lamb

What a scene had appeared before John's eyes! What a great victory was being celebrated! The Lion of the tribe of Judah is identified as the very Lamb of God who came to take away the sin of the world (Jn.1:29). However, what endears the Saviour to the hearts of His people is not His role as the Lion but that He is the precious Lamb of God. John the Baptist invited the people of his day to "behold" Him, and we must do just that. Have you looked, by faith, to Jesus? Have you asked Him to save you from your sins? Are you trusting in Him? Can you sing, from your heart, the majestic words of heaven's anthem, "Worthy is the Lamb that was slain to receive power, and riches, and wisdom, and strength, and honour, and glory, and blessing" (v.12)?

Some years ago I used to visit an elderly believer whose voice box had been removed. He was only able to speak by using a gadget that amplified what he said, but his heart was filled with praise. A favourite little saying of his was often repeated in conversation. I think he probably made the statement every time I saw him. Holding the gadget to his throat, he would say, "He is the Lamb for all eternity". How true! Throughout heaven's endless ages Jesus will be known and loved as the Lamb of God! He will never cease to be the Lamb. A little later in Revelation we meet "a great multitude" which is too vast to count, standing before the throne of God dressed in white robes and with palms of victory in their hands. Their song ascribes salvation to God who sits upon the throne and to the Lamb (Rev.7:9,10).

Praise God that the Lamb who died at Calvary is the Lion who rose triumphant from the grave! One day, if we belong to Him, we shall see Him in glory and shall know Him by the wounds of Calvary. He is at the centre of the scene of majesty and will be praised by His adoring people for ever.

Chapter 8
<u>No night there</u>

In the land of fadeless day
Lies "the city four-square";
It shall never pass away,
And there is "no night there."

God shall "wipe away all tears";
There's no death, no pain, nor fears;
And they count not time by years,
For there is "no night there".

All the gates of pearl are made
In "the city four-square";

All the streets with gold are laid,
And there is "no night there".

And the gates shall never close
To "the city four-square",
There life's crystal river flows,
And there is "no night there".

There they need no sunshine bright
In "the city four-square";
For the Lamb is all the light,
And there is "no night there".

John R. Clements

We have already seen that one of the figures used in the New Testament to help us understand heaven is a city. Abraham, you may recall, was looking for a city that had been built and made by God (Heb.11:10). Called by God, Abraham had left Ur of the Chaldees (Gen.11:28) and had embarked upon a pilgrimage to an unknown destination. Ur would have been very different from the enormous sprawling cities that we are familiar with today. Archaeology can only tell us in a limited way what the cities in Abraham's time were really like. But the patriarch had *another* city in his mind's eye. What kind of a picture he had, we can only imagine. All we are told in the sacred text is that his spiritual eye was focused upon it and that it had foundations. It was no ethereal or imaginary destiny but was *real*. It had a secure foundation and was built by God Himself. No terrestrial city has ever been built by God, so Abraham was not looking for any place on earth.

91

Another verse in Hebrews speaks of this city. We read in Hebrews 13:14: "For here have we no continuing city, but we seek one to come." The cities that we are familiar with today *seem* permanent enough. They may have been redeveloped and modernized during their history, but we cannot imagine them simply disappearing. If disaster strikes and an earthquake destroys its buildings, work will soon be done to repair the damage and make things even safer than they were before. But the writer of Hebrews points out that here on earth God's people have "no continuing city" — or no permanent home. Instead, we are seeking a city that lies ahead. That city is the very one Abraham was intent on finding. Like him, we ought to *seek* it. Our minds and affections ought to be set upon it. We should be thinking of heaven *now*. We need to distance ourselves from the things of earth.

How do we "seek" this heavenly city, and where can it be found? We learn of it in the Word of God and find a fascinating description of it at the end of Revelation. In this chapter we are going to examine John's account of it as recorded in Revelation 21. Perhaps not every detail should be interpreted literally because John was being shown things from another realm. The only way in which he could understand *anything* about heaven was by its features being conveyed to him in terms with which he was familiar. Thus the heavenly city is described in terms of an earthly city; but it is presented as a city far more wonderful than anything with which we are familiar. In this description we shall see *the sanctity of the city*, for the place itself and its inhabitants are characterized by holiness. We are also told a number of things about *the structure of the city* and how it is constructed. Finally, the whole description makes us aware of *the supremacy of the city* because it surpasses in beauty anything known upon earth.

One of the seven angels to whom had been entrusted the seven bowls filled with the wrath of God came and spoke to John. He had been assigned with the task of revealing "the bride, the Lamb's wife" (v.9) to him. In order to see this, John needed to be transported to "a great and high mountain" where he saw "that great city, the holy Jerusalem" descending from the abode of God (v.9,10). An elevated position was necessary for John to appreciate the scene that was about to be unveiled before his eyes. This introduces to us the first feature of our study:—

The Sanctity of the City

John himself was able to witness "the holy city, new Jerusalem" coming down out of heaven, from God, "prepared as a bride adorned for her husband" (v.2). It was therefore a picture of great beauty. Think of a young bride on her wedding day. It is an occasion that she has anticipated with excitement. She wants to look her very best for the one she loves and is to marry. Guests at the wedding often admire the beautiful dress and the bouquet that the bride is carrying. Everything has been carefully planned.

The "bride" that John sees (the *holy city*) is a picture of great beauty. It is not the *earthly* city of Jerusalem but is distinctly *heavenly*. The fact that the city descends "from God *out of heaven*" [emphasis added] indicates that it is not identical to heaven. As a city it is holy because all its inhabitants are holy. Sinful people are completely excluded from its streets (see verse 8). Earlier, in Revelation 17, we find an absolute contrast. Another woman is pictured there — a gaudily-painted harlot. In her repulsive and artificial state she represents apostate religion. But the city of Revelation 21 represents the true Church, the Redeemed of the Lord, as a body of people. Seven local congregations were seen, earlier, upon earth, in the second and third chapters of Revelation. The failings of the members of those congregations were patently obvious then, but no imperfections are seen in the "holy city" that John beholds!

93

"That great city, the holy Jerusalem," possesses the glory of God (v.10b,11a). From the description given, it appears not to descend to the earth but rather to hover *over* the earth. Piecing together the three figures used, the *bride* speaks of love, while the *wife* suggests a helper (seen from Genesis 2:18). The idea of a *city* perhaps conveys the thought of administration, for a city needs to be organized to run efficiently. Overall, however, we cannot escape from the holiness of this community. Nothing unclean can ever enter the city but only those people whose names have been recorded in the Lamb's book of life (v.27). Would we like to understand more about that holy place? Matthew Henry was right when he stated, "Those who would have clear views of heaven must get as near heaven as they can." Like John, who was carried to that "great and high mountain," we must live near to the Lord in order to breathe the pure air of heaven.

Not only were John's eyes employed; his ears were used too. "A great voice" was heard from heaven (v.3). This was nothing to keep quiet about! It was a moment of triumph! "Behold, the tabernacle of God is with men," the angelic messenger declared, "and He will dwell with them." Centuries before, there had been a literal "tabernacle" on earth to signify the presence of God. In fact, He had promised to "set [His] tabernacle among [them]" and to "walk among" His people. If they were obedient to His commands, they would enjoy the awareness of His presence and would know that they were His people and that He was their God (Lev.26:11,12).

When the tabernacle was replaced by the magnificent temple, Solomon longed for the presence of God too. But He knew that God Almighty could not be confined to any earthly sanctuary. If the very "heaven of heavens" could not contain Him, how much less could any man-made structure (1 Kings 8:27)! Yet here in Revelation 21 we find that aspiration fulfilled. God is seen to be "tabernacling" with His people and enjoying a perfect relationship with them. A foretaste of this was known when the Lord Jesus came to earth and (literally) "pitched His tent" among us (Jn.1:14). His very name Emmanuel means "God with us" (Mt.1:23). As we conclude this section, we might well ask how it is possible for God to dwell among men. It is only because of the sanctity of the city. A holy God can only dwell among a *people* who are made holy.

The Structure of the City

In the vision he was given, John was able to appreciate something of the *design* of the city. He noticed a wall that was "great and high" with twelve gates that were guarded by twelve angels (v.12). The idea of both a wall and angels speaks to us of protection. Each of the twelve gates was linked with one of the tribes of Israel, presumably suggesting that a particular tribe would find access through the gate bearing its name. The number *twelve* in Scripture appears to speak of government.

The city was designed in such a way that there was a perfect balance. Three gates on each side afforded access, the gates leading to each of the four points of the compass (v.13). The message of the gospel is proclaimed across the globe, and sinners in their need are invited to come to the Saviour. But not only is access possible with people from all parts of the world being allowed *in*. There is also the thought here of blessing flowing *out* from the city in all directions.

Something else about the city's wall was noticed by John. It possessed twelve foundations that were linked to "the twelve apostles of the Lamb" (v.14). The city was therefore perfectly secure in structure. Abraham, as we have seen, was seeking this very city with foundations, built by God Himself (Heb.11:10). Thinking of those foundations and the "apostles of the Lamb", we can recall the fact that the Church of the Lord Jesus Christ has been built upon the foundation of those apostles (Eph.2:20). They were instrumental in beginning the ministry which has created that body of believing people known as the Church (Eph.1:23). We notice, however, that the apostles have not replaced those twelve tribes — for they are still remembered at the gates of the city. The wall of the city, we observe, is made of jasper (a translucent stone), while the city itself is constructed of pure gold which is as clear as glass (v.18).

Having taken notice of the main features of the city, John's attention was drawn to more specific details. The foundations (linked, as we have seen, to the twelve apostles of the Lamb) were adorned with all kinds of precious stones which are listed by John. Such costly *decoration* adds to our appreciation of the city. Jasper, which we have already mentioned, was found in the first foundation. It is a stone that is connected with the throne of God. Sapphire (lapis lazuli) is a blue stone, the colour of the sky. It is next in hardness to a diamond. We find it used in the high priest's breastplate of old. The third precious stone was chalcedony, a green silicate of copper. Next could be seen emerald, a light-green coloured gem. The fifth stone listed is sardonyx, consisting of a layer of red sard and white onyx. This particular stone was much prized by the Romans. The sixth was sardius, a brilliant stone that is either yellowy-brown in colour or transparent red. Chrysolyte, the seventh stone, is golden and rather like topaz, while beryl (the eighth gem) is a sea-green transparent stone. The ninth stone, topaz, is golden-yellow and is almost as hard as diamond. It possesses the power of double refraction and when heated or rubbed becomes electric. Chrysoprasus, listed next, is a translucent golden-green stone. The eleventh is jacinth, a dark blue iris colour. Our English word *hyacinth* is related to this, and the gem probably resembles a sapphire. The final stone in the list is amethyst, a "wine-coloured" stone that literally means "not drunken"!

Many wonderful truths that are beyond the scope of this chapter (and beyond the grasp of the author!) could surely be gleaned from these gems. So many of them feature in the high priest's breastplate, which is described in the book of Exodus. As we think of their properties, we can appreciate that (generally speaking) light is either reflected by the stones or allowed to shine through them. Surely, as we consider them together, they speak to us of the glories of Christ. Combined, their blended colours may resemble the rainbow.

Before concluding our look at the decoration of the city, there are a few other features that must be noted. Each of the twelve gates was made out of pearl, but each gate was made simply from one enormous pearl (v.21). As those gates were large enough to allow access, how utterly enormous those pearls must have been! Pearls come from the sea and are formed when an irritant makes its way into an oyster. Beauty is thus produced through suffering. How immense the suffering must have been to produce a pearl the size of a gate! Surely this speaks to us of what our sinless Redeemer, the Lord Jesus Christ, suffered as He endured the agonies of the cross to save our souls! The street of the city, however, was made from gold that resembled transparent glass (v.21b). The streets of our cities today are often filthy. Rubbish and dirt easily accumulate, and regular cleaning must be undertaken in order to preserve the good "image" of a pleasant city. The heavenly city will be nothing like that! Gold speaks of divine righteousness. In that city all will be pure and transparent, and there will be nothing to hide.

The angel entrusted with showing the glories of the city to John was equipped with a golden reed with which its *dimensions* could be measured (v.15). The fact that the reed was made of gold indicates to us that divine and righteous standards were being used. The city is described as being "foursquare", with its length, breadth, and height being equal in size (v.16). "Twelve thousand furlongs" (the specified distance) equates to fifteen hundred miles. Sceptics sometimes question how big heaven must be if believers from across the world who have lived over many centuries are to be accommodated there. Imagine a city that is 1,500 miles in length and 1,500 miles in breadth — as well as being 1,500 miles in height! (The city appears to resemble a cube.) There is hardly going to be a problem of enough space when those dimensions are understood!

The equal proportions are surely intended to teach us a practical lesson. So often now we "get things out of proportion", stressing one particular truth and neglecting another. Not then! Perfect balance will be appreciated, and enjoyed.

The wall itself was 144 cubits in thickness (v.17). There is some debate as to whether a cubit is eighteen inches or nearer to twenty-four inches. Allowing for the lower figure, the wall of the city must have been at least 200 feet thick; perhaps as much as 240 feet! This might seem enormous, but when we remember that the wall extended 1,500 miles in one direction the thickness is appropriate. We can well be impressed by this description of the heavenly city. It is so unlike anything that we know upon earth. This brings us to the third section of this present chapter.

The Supremacy of the City

The first thing we can say is that such a place is *preferable* to any earthly city! Some folk nowadays enjoy a "city break" — visiting a city of historic or cultural interest and exploring its ancient streets and buildings. This heavenly city surpasses them all! In some historic cities you may find ancient temples or church buildings, but in the heavenly city no temple can be found. There is a good reason for this. Earthly cities have their religious buildings because men imagine that those who enter a sacred building are somehow closer to God. Nobody in heaven needs to get nearer to God, for all are equally near. That is why "the Lord God Almighty and the Lamb are the temple of it" (v.22).

Earthly cities unquestionably need street lighting. Every so often the lighting is improved and the effects of light are enhanced, but in the heavenly city there is nothing of this kind. Greater than the light of the sun or of the moon are the glories which shine from God and the

Lamb and illuminate the city (v.23). Unlike ancient cities where the gates were shut and locked at night to keep undesirable people out, the gates of heaven remain open perpetually. Criminal activities usually flourish in the hours of darkness, but as far as the heavenly city is concerned "there shall be no night there" (v.25). God is glorified in all the activities of the city, and all uncleanness is excluded. Only the redeemed, whose names are recorded in the Lamb's book of life, have access to the city (v.26,27).

When we put all such aspects together, how much better the city is than anything with which we are familiar now! Nothing that defiles ... nothing abominable ... nothing untrue will be found in the city. Often today tourists in a foreign city can be deceived and taken advantage of by unscrupulous traders, but nothing of that kind will ever happen in the heavenly city! All of this makes the place far more preferable to anything that can be known now.

In addition to this, the city is a *pleasurable* location. John was shown "a pure river of water of life, clear as crystal, proceeding out of the throne of God and of the Lamb" (Rev.22:1). Many earthly cities have been built on the banks of rivers in order to utilise the flowing water which has generated power and provided a means of transportation. However, rivers flowing near to places of industry and human occupation can often be polluted and dirty — but not there! That which emanates from God's throne is pure and unadulterated. "The tree of life" which was known in Eden also flourishes here. It offers a constant supply of fruit that is unaffected by seasonal variations. Our apple trees only bear fruit in their season and for much of the year are without apples, but in the heavenly city the tree of life is productive "every month" (22:2). The luscious fruit from the tree of life has healing properties too.

Wonderfully, "there shall be no more curse" (22:3). How the curse of God, pronounced in Eden because of Adam's sin, has blighted our world! But there the curse will be lifted and life will be transformed. The throne of God and of the Lamb is found there, and His servants will have unrestricted access into His presence as they engage in His service. A mark on the forehead identified the cursed of earth who had given their allegiance to the Beast of Revelation 13, but here the people of God bear His own mark upon their foreheads (22:3,4). "And they shall see his face ..." (v.4). Centuries before our time, David had longed for the moment when he would behold that face in righteousness and would awake "satisfied" in His presence (Ps.17:15). If we belong to the Lord and are His children we, too, shall "see him as he is" (1 Jn.3:2).

What a day that will be! No night will end the eternal day. No artificial illumination will be needed to dispel any lingering darkness. The people of God shall reign with Him "for ever and ever" (22:5). What more is needed? The scene is triumphant. Who can doubt the supremacy of this city, surpassing (as it does) the splendour of anything that we know on earth.

"No night there"

What a wonderful city has been before us in this chapter! The two chapters with which Revelation closes present the most fitting conclusion to the Word of God that anyone might have written. But I want us to draw these thoughts to an end on a practical note by remembering a statement recorded in Philippians.

The word translated "conversation" refers to *citizenship* and appears as such in other versions of the Bible. "Our conversation [citizenship] is in heaven; from whence also we look for the Saviour, the Lord Jesus Christ, who shall change our vile [i.e. lowly] body, that it may be fashioned like unto his glorious body, according to the working whereby he is able even to subdue all things unto himself" (Phil.3:20,21). Put simply, we are citizens of heaven and do not really belong upon earth. Because of our connection with that other world, we look for the Saviour who is going to come *from* heaven. When He comes, He is going to radically alter these poor mortal bodies of ours by His mighty power. We shall be changed completely and given bodies of glory that resemble His.

What makes these verses practical? The answer is that the Lord wants us to *live* as citizens of heaven *now!* As Peter reminds us in 1 Peter 2:11, we are "strangers and pilgrims" upon earth. As strangers we do not belong, and as pilgrims we are journeying somewhere else. Does this not remind us of Abraham, the pilgrim? He "looked for a city" (Heb.11:10), and we "look for the Saviour" (Phil.3:20) who is coming *from* that city to take us there to be with Him. Let us never forget: we are going somewhere far, far better!

Chapter 9

No more Tents!

"For ever with the Lord!"
Amen, so let it be!
Life from the dead is in that word,
'Tis immortality.
Here in the body pent,
Absent from Him I roam,
Yet nightly pitch my moving tent
A day's march nearer home.

My Father's house on high,
Home of my soul, how near
At times to faith's foreseeing eye
Thy golden gates appear!
Ah! then my spirit faints
To reach the land I love,
The bright inheritance of saints,
Jerusalem above.

"For ever with the Lord!"
Father, if 'tis Thy will,
The promise of that faithful word
E'en here to me fulfil.
Be Thou at my right hand,
Then can I never fail;
Uphold Thou me, and I shall stand;
Fight, and I must prevail.

So when my latest breath
Shall rend the veil in twain,
By death I shall escape from death,
And life eternal gain.
That resurrection-word,
That shout of victory:
Once more, "For ever with the Lord!"
Amen, so let it be!

James Montgomery

Voyager 1 is a space probe that was launched by NASA on the 5th September, 1977, to study the solar system. After passing the planets Jupiter and Saturn, and exploring the weather and magnetic fields of Titan (Saturn's large moon) the probe continued its unbelievable journey into outer space. On the 20th November, 1980, *Voyager 1* began its exploration of the heliosphere (the enormous, bubble-like region of space that is dominated by the sun and extends beyond Pluto). Another milestone was reached in 2012 when (on the 25th August) *Voyager 1* crossed the heliopause and entered interstellar space. The mission is planned to continue until 2025, by which time the space probe's instruments will no longer have enough electrical power to operate.

How incredible it is to think that a space probe can travel so far and so fast and yet can remain in contact with NASA's Deep Space Network for close on fifty years! Space itself is vast and measureless.

We cannot comprehend infinity any more than we can understand eternity. To be able to grasp with our minds something that is endless (whether in time or in distance) is utterly beyond us. Yet, as Christian believers, many concepts that are impossible to explain by reason and logic can still be accepted by faith.

According to the teaching of the Bible, when believers leave this world they go to heaven. *How* this is possible, we cannot explain — but we have reason to believe it. At the funeral of a true Christian we are often reminded that the departed soul has gone to be with Christ, which is far better (Phil.1:23). But the coffin before us proves that it can only be in *spirit* that the departed person is with the Lord. Within that coffin lies the body in which the soul and spirit once lived. However, that body is not entirely finished with. We learn from God's Word that a day of resurrection lies ahead, not the resurrection of our spirits but of our *bodies*. God's people who are already with Him are only there in spirit, but His purpose is that they should be with Him *in body* as well. This is what we are going to consider in this chapter, and we shall develop the subject under four headings.

The Promise of Resurrection

The promise of resurrection was expressed by the Lord Jesus. "Marvel not at this," He declared; "for the hour is coming, in the which all that are in the graves shall hear his voice, and shall come forth; they that have done good, unto the resurrection of life; and they that have done evil, unto the resurrection of damnation" (Jn.5:28,29). The disciples might have been surprised, but they were not to be. At the sound of the Lord's voice *all* who have passed away will be raised from death. None can escape the summoning call. A little later in John's gospel we see the authority of the Lord Jesus when He called Lazarus forth from the tomb (Jn.11:43). That mighty act of power is a tangible demonstration of what will most certainly take place when the dead are raised — but not all will be raised at the same time. "The resurrection of life" is for *believers* only and will take place first. At a later time there will be "the resurrection of damnation" when those who have died in unbelief will be raised to face Christ as judge and to be condemned for having never done the "good" thing, which means having never repented of their sins and trusted Him for salvation.

Someone might say, "I can understand, up to a point, the raising of Lazarus to continued life on this earth. But I cannot fathom the transporting of human bodies to heaven. How could such a thing ever happen?" We have a preview of that coming event in the ascension of the Lord Jesus to heaven. Before the gaze of His own disciples, after having spoken to them, Jesus was parted from them and carried up into heaven. They watched Him ascend into the skies until a cloud hid Him from their sight. His departure was followed immediately by the arrival of two angels who declared that "this same Jesus" who had been taken from them would return from heaven in just the same way (Acts 1:9—11). Just as He was "taken up" from the earth, His people will be carried up to heaven too! It is all expressed as a very *natural* promise.

But not only is the promise to be understood naturally. It is also a very *necessary* promise, as we see from 1 Corinthians 15. "As we have borne the image of the earthy, we shall also bear the image of the heavenly" (1 Cor.15:49). The "earthy" refers Adam, the man who was created from the dust of the ground. We all bear his "image" in that we are his descendants. But those who are saved are going to "bear the image of the heavenly" — referring to the Lord Jesus

Christ, the Man from heaven. We shall be like Him, one day.

At the present time we consist of "flesh and blood" and cannot, in that state, inherit the kingdom of God. Our bodies, when they die, face "corruption" and cannot enter a realm that is characterized by "incorruption" and perfect holiness. We need to be radically changed — and changed we shall be! Paul reveals "a mystery" to us; this means a truth that had not been revealed before and could only be known by divine revelation. "We shall not all sleep," he declared, "but we shall all be changed" (1 Cor.15:50,51). Not all believers are going to die because the Lord is returning in the lifetime of some. But all believers need to be changed in order to enter heaven.

I heard an amusing story about someone who was looking for a card to mark the arrival of a new baby. The person wanted to send the baby's parents a card containing a Bible verse, so he began to look through the "New Baby" section where cards were displayed. As he looked, he came across a card with a most unusual verse inside. It contained the words quoted earlier, "We shall not all sleep, but we shall all be changed"!! If you have had any experience of new-born babies you will know only too well that they do not sleep all the time, but they *do* all need to be changed regularly!

While the verse was being used in the wrong context in a card of this kind, the lesson is clear. We *do* need to be changed. When the Lord Jesus returns from heaven with that summoning shout, the dead will be raised and the living will rise to meet Him in the air. *All* will be changed, both the dead and the living. Our present bodies face corruption through death and need to become incorruptible. This mortal frame, which of necessity must succumb to death, needs to be made immortal (1 Cor.15:52,53). These things are absolutely *necessary* for us and are part of the promise of resurrection found in Scripture. They will most certainly come to pass.

The Proof of Resurrection

The great "resurrection chapter" (1 Corinthians 15) expresses the concept of resurrection, firstly, as a *fact*. Not only did the Lord Jesus die upon the cross; after His burial in the tomb He was raised from the dead on the third day, "according to the Scriptures" (v.4). The resurrection of Christ is integral to the message of the gospel. In the early part of the chapter Paul furnishes further proof and lists a number of witnesses who saw the risen Christ. This leads to the triumphant conclusion in verse 20, "But now is Christ risen from the dead." Not only did He rise from the dead, but He remains in that risen state. It is not simply that He has risen but that He *continues* in that same risen life. Believers rejoice when they remember the death of the Lord Jesus because He is now alive for ever! Before experiencing the agonies of the cross, He said to His disciples: "Because I live, ye shall live also" (Jn.14:19). He wants His saints to live with Him, and this can only be possible when they are changed and taken beyond death.

In 1 Corinthians 15 we find that the doctrine of resurrection is not simply expressed as a *fact*: it is also explained in a *figure*. The verse quoted previously states that Christ has "become the firstfruits of them that slept" (v.20). The "firstfruits" comprise the first part of the harvest. They are not the *whole* harvest but are just the first part of it. However, they are also the proof that more will follow. Paul uses an analogy to explain this to us. "For since by man came death, by man came also the resurrection of the dead" (v.21). Adam was the man responsible for introducing death to the human race. Another "man" ("the man Christ Jesus" [1 Tim.2:5]) has introduced resurrection by being its "firstfruits" — the first to rise from death never to die again. "For as in Adam all die, even so in Christ shall all be made alive" (v.22). Death has terminated the life of every human being (apart from Enoch and Elijah) since Adam; but those who are "in Christ" through salvation shall be "made alive" at His coming. "But every man in his own order: Christ the firstfruits; afterward they that are Christ's at his coming" (v.23). The correct sequence must be followed. Just as the firstfruits precede the full harvest, so Christ's own resurrection from the dead precedes what will happen at His return when the believing dead will be raised. This explains the phrase, "but every man in his own order".

This teaching is confirmed in 2 Corinthians 4:14: "Knowing that he which raised up the Lord Jesus shall raise up us also by Jesus, and shall present us with you." Paul assures his readers that we *know* this truth. God the Father raised up His own Son on the third day and will also raise His people from death in a coming day. All believers will be presented together ("us with you") in glory.

Returning to 1 Corinthians 15, another figure is employed by Paul later in the chapter. This time he considers the sowing of a seed in the soil. The seed may look dull and uninteresting and may appear to be lifeless, but when it dies in the soil and germinates it springs forth as a vibrant, fresh new shoot. Similarly, the body that is "sown" in death is a "natural body" but is raised as a "spiritual body". The body that is laid to rest in the grave is "sown in corruption" and is going to decay, but when it is raised it will be as an incorruptible body. Placed within the grave is a body that is characterized by "dishonour" and may have shown signs of age or illness, but it will be raised in glory. It is "sown in weakness" as a mortal body that was impotent to overcome death, but it will be "raised in power" — triumphant over death (v.42—44).

This figure from nature teaches us about resurrection. Like a plant growing from a seed, we shall rise to enter a new life. But the greatest proof is surely the resurrection of Christ Himself. Because He was raised from the dead, His people will rise to glory too!

The Purpose of Resurrection

In seeking to understand the purpose of resurrection, there are two expressions that we need to consider. The first of these is *translation*. The closing verses of 1 Thessalonians 4 run parallel to the final part of 1 Corinthians 15 and deal with the return of the Lord Jesus from heaven. In this passage we learn that when believers die, those who are left behind can live in hope. We do not sorrow as people might do when an unbeliever dies because, for them, there is no hope after death. "If" (or "since") we believe that Jesus died and also rose from the dead, those who have died believing in Him will be raised too.

With the authority of an apostle to whom "the word of the Lord" had been revealed, Paul declared that those who are alive when the Lord Jesus returns will not precede into His presence those who have already died. "For the Lord Himself shall descend from heaven with a shout" — accompanied by the sound of the archangel's voice and the trumpet-call of God. When this happens, those who have died believing in Jesus will rise first; then those who are still living and know Him as Saviour will also be caught up "together with them in the clouds" in order to meet the Lord who has returned in the air (1 Thess.4:13—17). The prospect thrilled the poet James Montgomery whose triumphant hymn *For ever with the Lord* is printed at the beginning of this chapter. We may well respond, "Amen, so let it be!"

Remember, according to 1 Corinthians 15:51, "we shall not all sleep." Some will be *living* when Christ returns from heaven to call His Church to be with Him. Christ is the source of our life, and when He returns from heaven in splendour His people will share His glory (Col.3:4). In order for that to take place we need the promised resurrection to effect our translation into His presence.

The second expression that must be understood is *transformation*. Earlier in this book we have examined Philippians 3:20,21 and have seen that, as heavenly citizens, we are awaiting the return of our Lord Jesus Christ. When He comes from heaven He will transform these lowly bodies of ours and fashion them like His own body of glory by means of the power whereby He is able to subdue all things unto Himself. Other Scriptures confirm this divine purpose. John tells us that we shall see the Lord Jesus *as He is* and shall be made like Him (1 Jn.3:2). What a transformation that will be!

How long will the work require in order for it to take place? It will happen "in a moment" (1 Cor.15:52). The Greek word *atomos* (used here) gives us our word "atom" and refers to that which is indivisible. How small is an atom? Have you ever wondered how many atoms there might be in one drop of water? The number would be too large to print and would mean very little to us in any case. There are billions of trillions of atoms in one drop of water, and in just one of those "atoms" (which cannot be divided) we shall be changed! So part of the purpose of this coming resurrection is our transformation.

The Prospect of Resurrection

It is vital to have the prospect of resurrection before us. In the previous section we referred to 1 John 3:2 and to being made like the Lord Jesus when we see Him as He is. The next verse says, "And every man that hath this hope in him purifieth himself, even as he is pure" (1 Jn.3:3). The hope of the Lord's return and of being with Him ought to have a sanctifying effect upon our lives. Knowing that He is coming again at any moment will encourage holy living.

The theme of His return features prominently in 1 Thessalonians. Each chapter of that epistle ends with a reference to His coming again, and on some occasions practical exhortations are given. We are waiting for God's Son from heaven who will deliver us from the coming wrath of God (1 Thess.1:10). "For what is our hope, or joy, or crown of rejoicing?" asks Paul as he considers his ministry at

Thessalonica. "Are not even ye in the presence of our Lord Jesus Christ at his coming?" (1 Thess.2:19). They mattered to him, and he wanted to see them complete in Christ at His coming and ready to share in His glory. As he pondered that coming day, Paul's great concern was that the hearts of God's people at Thessalonica should be established in holiness and that they should be without blame before Him (1 Thess.3:13). Again his concern was that God would do a work in holiness *now* that would remain and would be seen *then*. The Lord Jesus Christ died for us "that, whether we wake or sleep, we should live together with him" (1 Thess.5:10).

Whether we are alive on earth at Christ's coming or not, is immaterial. His purpose is that "together with him" we should *live*. All of these thoughts in Scripture are intended to have a sanctifying effect upon our lives.

The coming of Christ should also be a *satisfying* prospect. If we love the Lord, we should have within our hearts a longing to be with Him. In our lives, now, there are often trials and difficulties that are hard to bear. We can find ourselves burdened with troubles — and many dear believers today are suffering greatly for their faith. Weighing this up, and considering what lies ahead, Paul declared: "For I reckon that the sufferings of this present time are not worthy to be compared with the glory which shall be revealed in us" (Rom.8:18). *Glory* lies ahead! We cannot understand how dazzling it will be. But Paul is not writing about the glory that is to be revealed *to* us. The statement distinctly contrasts "the sufferings of this present time" with *the glory that is to be revealed in us* — in these bodies that the Lord has redeemed for Himself. The whole of creation, it would appear, somehow waits with eager anticipation for the moment when the sons of God will be manifested (Rom.8:19). What a prospect that will be!

Paul, as an ardent believer, was not complacent in his Christian walk.

He pressed on "toward the mark" as he focused his spiritual gaze on the coming again of the Lord Jesus and the moment when His people will appear in His presence (Phil.3:14). He is coming "to be glorified in his saints, and to be admired in all them that believe … in that day" (2 Thess.1:10). Yes, He will be glorified *in* the lives of His believing people when He comes again.

In 2 Corinthians 5 Paul compares the human body to a tent. If this earthly "tabernacle" is taken down, he declared, there is another home prepared for us — not a tent, but a "building" that is "eternal in the heavens" (v.1). While we are "at home" [living] in this body, "we are absent from the Lord" (v.6). This is not what we really want. Our real ambition is to be "absent from the body and … present with the Lord" (v.6;8). It does not give us pleasure to be absent from Him now, living (as we are) in what James Montgomery calls "this moving tent"! We long to leave our present temporal abode and be truly "at home" with the Lord.

Imagine living in a tent for any length of time. For a start, you would find conditions very cramped with little room to move around. Potentially it would also be a damp and draughty place — particularly if the changeable (and frequently disappointing) British weather is in mind. Also, tents are not always the quietest of places! The rain falling on the canvas in the night and the sound of early morning traffic can mean that sleep is often disturbed. But imagine being able to move into a comfortable and spacious house after spending a year or two in a tent! "It's so much better!" you would exclaim. "It's just wonderful to be able to stand upright and walk around freely. There is so much space in this house! I'm feeling a lot healthier, too. The dampness made me cough, and I was frequently cold. At night the draught could not be kept out when the bitter wind was blowing. What a blessing, too, to have solid brick walls and not flapping canvas! It's all so much quieter. Living in a tent was a novelty for a few days, but I'm so much better off in this comfortable house. I wouldn't want to go back to living in a tent again for anything!"

The contrast could hardly be greater, but it is the illustration that Paul uses when comparing life in the human body upon earth now with the "resurrection body" that God has for His people in heaven. Centuries before, David declared, "I shall be satisfied, when I awake, with thy likeness" (Ps.17:15). Each redeemed child of God would re-echo those words. The prospect of being beyond death and in His eternal presence is the most satisfying one we could imagine.

"For ever with the Lord!"

The words of that hymn bring us towards the conclusion of this chapter. *For ever with the Lord! Amen, so let it be!* That is our prospect. Our Saviour died for our sins that we might live eternally in His presence. We are not morbidly waiting for death!

The word *cemetery* literally means "a dormitory" — and in this case it refers to a place where the body sleeps until resurrection. But death is not our destiny! We are going to leave this scene of time to be "with Christ" which is far, far better (Phil.1:23). However, we are not there yet. We still live in these tent-like structures that are mortal and eventually wear out. Shortly before his death, John Knox said, "Live in Christ, die in Christ, and the flesh need not fear." The certainty of the truths of Scripture that have been before us in this chapter should help to dispel those fears. In the meanwhile may we seek to "glorify God" in our mortal bodies, because they have been redeemed and therefore rightly belong to Him (1 Cor.6:20).

Chapter 10

Heaven – My Home

I'm but a stranger here,
Heaven is my home;
Only a sojourner,
Heaven is my home:
Danger and sorrow stand
Round me on every hand;
Heaven is my Fatherland,
Heaven is my home.

What though the tempest rage,
Heaven is my home!
Short is my pilgrimage,
Heaven is my home:
And time's wild, wintry blast
Soon will be over-past:
I shall reach home at last,
Heaven is my home.

There at my Saviour's side,
Heaven is my home!
I shall be glorified,
Heaven is my home:
There are the good and blest,
Those I love most and best,
And there I too shall rest,
Heaven is my home.

Therefore I'll murmur not,
Heaven is my home;
Whate'er my earthly lot,
Heaven is my home:
For I shall surely stand
There at my Lord's right hand;
Heaven is my Fatherland,
Heaven is my home.

T. R. Taylor

In his first epistle to the Thessalonians the apostle Paul wrote, "And so shall we ever be with the Lord" (1 Thess.4:17). What triumphant words these are! James Montgomery used them in the opening line of his hymn *For ever with the Lord!* (quoted in chapter 9) which is frequently chosen to be sung at a believer's funeral service. We find it impossible to comprehend what it will mean to be with the Lord eternally, for eternity is a concept far beyond the grasp of our finite minds. Nevertheless we believe that which is written in the Word of God.

LIFE BEYOND THE SUNSET

The previous chapters of this book have taken us on a journey through Scripture. We have approached *life beyond the sunset* from a number of different angles — thinking of heaven in terms of a city, a home, and paradise (a beautiful garden). In this chapter we shall tie up some loose ends and consider just a few of the many features of life in heaven that we could explore. Frankly, we can only scratch the surface. So many books have been written about heaven, and this short book is by no means *the* definitive publication! There is so much more that could have been written within these covers; but at the same time there is also so much that we simply *do not know* about heaven.

If we are Christian believers who have been saved by the Lord Jesus Christ, we are on our way to heaven. In an earlier chapter we pondered Proverbs 4:18 and saw how "the path of the just is as the shining light, that shineth more and more unto the perfect day." Those who have been made righteous by the Lord Jesus Christ are walking ahead into the light. We are not going out into the darkness! The pathway that we are treading, according to God's Word, grows ever brighter until we reach the land of perfect day. But as we journey we must remember than we are "strangers and pilgrims" who do not belong in this world (1 Pet.2:11). It is vital that we are aware of the "fleshly lusts" which, according to this verse, wage war against the soul. We must focus our spiritual gaze upon the Great Captain of our salvation, the Lord Jesus Christ, who has gone before us. We need to be "looking unto Jesus" as we travel home (Heb.12:2).

What lies ahead at the end of the journey? What will we discover when we arrive at the "perfect day" that awaits us? There are four topics that we shall consider in this chapter. First, we must give some thought to *relationships* in heaven. What will they be like? Second, we shall examine the subject of *rewards* — for the Bible speaks of these. Third, we shall listen to the *rejoicing* that can be heard in heaven, before considering finally what Scripture has to say about the saints of God *reigning* in heaven.

Relationships in Heaven

There can be no doubt that relationships in heaven will be *different* from what we know now. The Sadducees (who did not believe in the final resurrection of the body) raised a hypothetical question one day concerning a woman whose husband had died. The two of them had had no children. Following the bereavement, the woman (in accordance with Old Testament law) married one of her deceased husband's brothers. He also died leaving no offspring. The woman married once more, but the same happened again. In fact, she married seven different brothers in the same family before she also died. She was childless in each marriage. The Sadducees wanted to know which of the seven brothers would be married to her "in the resurrection" — for clearly she could not be married to all seven at once!

The Lord Jesus exposed the folly of His questioners. He knew that their question was designed to "trick" Him. *They*, however, were the ones in error because they knew not the Scriptures, nor the power of God! Had they studied the Scriptures they would have discovered truths about the resurrection life, but they were fettered by their own unbelief which denied any possibility of resurrection. According to the Lord Jesus we do not *enter into* marriage relationships in heaven but are as the angels of God who do not marry or procreate. However, although new human relationships are not entered into, existing spiritual relationships *do* continue.

The question asked was irrelevant because it was asked in unbelief. We must believe the Scriptures (which are God-given) and must be assured that the power of God can perform what is utterly beyond our ability. The Lord Jesus taught that those who have died and have entered into the presence of God still enjoy a relationship with Him.

To confirm this, He drew their attention to the time when Moses heard the voice of God at the burning bush. On that occasion God identified Himself with the words, "I *am* [emphasis added] the God of Abraham, and the God of Isaac, and the God of Jacob." Notice that the Almighty did not say that He *was* their God. No, although they were all dead (as Moses knew only too well) they were alive in God's presence, and He was *still* their God. The spiritual relationship that had been established *remained*. Truly, "God is not the God of the dead, but of the living" (Mt.22:23—32).

Earlier in this book I suggested that in heaven believers will know one another. How will we *relate* to one another? Will earthly relationships continue? We know from Scripture that the marriage bond is *unto death* (Rom.7:2). Many bereaved believers find great comfort in anticipating being reunited with a beloved spouse or parent after death, and I certainly would not want to deprive anyone of such comfort. If we are believers, we *shall* meet again: of this there can be no doubt. But while earthly relationships are going to be different in heaven, we can be equally sure that there are going to be no regrets. Nobody will be disappointed there and long for the days of earth again.

Relationships in heaven will also be *divine*. That which is spiritual will surpass that which is physical. We sometimes wonder what will happen when saved members of the same family meet one another in heaven. How will we relate to one another? My father has passed on into the presence of the Lord. He died at just over ninety years of age. When we meet again he will *still* be my father, but the relationship will not be exactly the same as it was on earth.

Some, like Abraham, die "at a good old age ... and full of years" (Gen.25:8). Others die in their youth, or even as children. Will such differences be observed in heaven? We are not given the answer to this question in as many words, but we can be quite sure that those who died in old-age will not appear as *frail* people in heaven. There will not be the present distinctions with which we are so familiar, where one person is stronger and fitter than another. The Bible assures us that we are "partakers of the divine nature" (2 Pet.1:4) and will therefore resemble Christ in heaven. Gentile believers have been brought into blessing with Jewish believers and are thus "partakers of his promise in Christ by the gospel" (Eph.3:6). In that promise, earthly distinctions vanish away. Thus, in heaven, we shall be *more* conscious of *divine* relationships and of being one in Christ Jesus with *all* His people. God's eternal purpose is to "gather together in one all things in Christ" in that coming day (Eph.1:10). The Lord Jesus Christ will be central.

Rewards in Heaven

In many places in the New Testament we are made aware of God's provision of rewards for His people, but before any are bestowed there must be a divine *assessment* of His children. As the Lord's servants we are accountable to Him and are personally responsible for how we fill our lives.

This truth emerges in a number of our Lord's parables. Consider, for instance, the parable of the nobleman who went into a far country to receive a kingdom and then to return. Before leaving, he entrusted his servants with responsibilities to fulfil in his absence. After he had departed, the citizens of the country (*not* his servants) sent a message after him, saying, "We will not have this man to reign over us." True to his promise he returned and in due time dealt with his rebellious subjects, but first he called his servants in order to know how they had fared with what had been entrusted to them during his absence (Lk.19:11—15). The parable speaks powerfully of Christ our Master who is currently absent from this scene. While His servants are engaged in responsibilities for Him, the godless citizens of this rebellious world brazenly declare their hatred and refuse to submit to His rule.

119

In Romans 14:12 we are told plainly that "every one of us shall give account of himself to God." We need to allow the force of those words to impress themselves upon us. Nobody is excluded, for the verse speaks of "every one of us" as believers, without exception. We shall give account of *ourselves* (rather than giving account of another) and the account is given to *God*. The Lord will not need *my* help on that occasion when He assesses someone else! My thoughts and appraisal of another servant will count for absolutely nothing. The Lord, in His fathomless wisdom, will assess everything perfectly. Our works, as believers, will be tested by the fire of His discerning judgment (1 Cor.3:13).

Another verse of Scripture confirms that "we must all appear before the judgment seat of Christ" in order "that every one may receive the things done in his body ... whether it be good or bad" (2 Cor.5:10). We cannot escape this truth. *All* true believers will stand before the Master to give account of their lives and service. (This is *not* the "great white throne judgment" described in Revelation 20 in which the ungodly are judged and are condemned. To use a comparison which might help us to understand the difference, the "judgment seat of Christ" is not like a court trial. It is rather more like a show at a country village when home-produced goods are "judged" to determine their quality. The "judgment seat of Christ" is not a judgment concerning salvation — these people are saved already — but concerning our service and faithfulness.) An assessment of our lives, as believers, lies before us. We should therefore be very careful how we live our lives now.

The assessment will be followed by an *acknowledgement*. We may recall another parable told by the Lord Jesus where one servant was entrusted with five talents and another with two. When they stood before their master, both were able to declare that the investment had doubled; one now had ten talents, the other had four. Both, however, were commended in identical terms: "Well done, thou good and faithful servant: thou hast been faithful over a few things, I will make thee ruler over many things: enter thou into the joy of thy lord" (Mt.25:21–23). Faithfulness during a time of responsibility led to an acknowledgement of what was done well, as well as to further responsibility, and to joy.

This is not heavenly-minded teaching that has no earthly use! It is very practical, relevant, and challenging. Servants of an earthly master were exhorted by Paul to perform their duties "as to the Lord, and not to men." The instruction continued: "Knowing that whatsoever good thing any man doeth, the same shall he receive of the Lord, whether he be bond or free" (Eph.6:7,8). We are assured, therefore, that *the Lord* will reward faithful service that has been done as to Him. Employers were also reminded of *their* "Master ... in heaven" and of His scrupulously righteous justice (Eph.6:9).

According to James, the individual who overcomes trial and testing will receive "the crown of life" which the Lord has promised to those who love Him (Jas.1:12). Earlier we referred to the testing that will take place under the scrutinizing fires of God's judgment when we stand before Him. In 1 Corinthians 3:14,15 we are told that any work that survives the fire will be worthy of reward. However, if anyone's work is destroyed by the fire because it was worthless, the individual himself will suffer the loss of his works yet shall be saved — "as by fire". The picture is of somebody escaping from their burning home and losing all their possessions, but they still survive the blaze. It is therefore possible for somebody to be saved and yet have nothing from that saved life (in terms of works) that is of value to the Lord. However, for faithful service rewards *will* be given. Of course, it must be stressed that true servants will always see themselves as "unprofitable" labourers who have only done their duty (Lk.17:10). They will gladly cast their crowns before the Lamb (Rev.4:10).

Rejoicing in Heaven

In heaven there will be the *consummation* (or fulfilment) of our earthly joys. One of our Lord's parables concerned a man who laid on "a great supper" and invited many (Lk.14:16). It was intended to be a time of rejoicing. In Revelation 19:9 we read of the future "marriage supper of the Lamb" which will be an occasion of unbounded joy. We learn from Ephesians 5:25—27 that the Lamb's "bride" is the Church. The Lord Jesus intends to present the Church in glory in that coming day. He who loved the Church and gave Himself for it longs for His purchased Bride to be with Him. The note of rejoicing rings out clearly in Revelation 19: "Let us be glad and rejoice, and give honour to him: for the marriage of the Lamb is come" (v.7). John was instructed to write the words, "Blessed are they which are called unto the marriage supper of the Lamb" (v.9). It will be a time of great rejoicing!

We have a foretaste of those joys in the writings of Isaiah in the Old Testament. "Thou shalt no more be termed Forsaken: neither shall thy land any more be termed Desolate: but thou shalt be called Hephzibah [delightful], and thy land Beulah [married]: for the Lord delighteth in thee, and thy land shall be married" (Isa.62:4). What was promised to God's people of old is a foretaste of that which lies ahead: the Bride of the Lamb will rejoice in her marriage relationship to Him.

This analogy calls for our careful *contemplation* because a practical application is linked to this truth. Revelation 19:7,8 states: "The marriage of the Lamb is come, and his wife hath made herself ready. And to her was granted that she should be arrayed in fine linen, clean and white; for the fine linen is the righteousness of saints." How has the "wife" made herself ready? She is seen clothed in "fine linen" robes. There can be no doubt whatever that we are covered with Christ's righteousness on account of His death upon the cross. Nobody who appreciates the work of the Lord Jesus would dispute the fact that our title to glory is found in His sacrifice alone and not for one moment in our own merit. However, some commentators see another meaning in this expression. Revelation 14:13 reveals that those who die in the Lord are "blessed" and that "their works do follow them" as they rest from their earthly labours. Connecting this verse with Revelation 19:8, it has been suggested that the righteous acts of the saints (which were done *for* Christ, in *His* strength, and by His Spirit alone) are seen adorning the Bride as she stands in glory with Him. Whether or not this interpretation is accepted, it presents a real challenge to us now.

The Lord Jesus has cautioned us not to lay up treasures for ourselves upon earth where moth and rust corrupt and where thieves break in and steal. Instead we are to lay up treasures in heaven by investing in the life that lies ahead (Mt.6:19,20). We must not be like the rich farmer of Luke 12 who had great plans for himself and for his future but left God out of the equation and consequently died as a fool. It is patently true that "we brought nothing into this world, and it is certain we can carry nothing out" (1 Tim.6:7). Remember the rich young ruler who came to the Lord Jesus with a perplexing question but left His presence with a sad heart. The reason that he "went away grieved" was that he had great possessions which he loved more than the Lord (Mk.10:21,22). It follows that if we would be rejoicing when we stand with the Lord in glory, we must hold the things of earthly lightly now, rather than tightly.

Reigning in Heaven

In his epistle to the Ephesians Paul explains that in the ages to come God is going to demonstrate "the exceeding riches of his grace in his kindness toward us through Christ Jesus" (Eph.2:7). How rich that grace has been! We cannot fathom it adequately now.

Another verse declares, "That as sin hath reigned unto death, even so might grace reign through righteousness unto eternal life by Jesus

Christ our Lord" (Rom.5:21). Sin certainly "reigns" upon earth in this present age, but the verse assures us that in the time to come *grace* shall reign through righteousness. We are told that in God's future purposes "the saints shall judge the world" (1 Cor.6:2). The Corinthians were made aware of this stupendous fact because they were failing to deal adequately with disputes among themselves in the church. It is only God's grace that purposes such things. Of ourselves we are unfit for such responsibilities and have no rightful claim to duties of this kind. Yet His wondrous grace shares such a work with us as we reign with Him.

God's *glory* will also be displayed in that future day. The saints of God are pictured accompanying Christ as He appears "in glory" from heaven (Col.3:4). A triumphant scene is brought before us in Revelation 19:14. The Lord Jesus Christ is pictured riding upon a white horse as He returns to earth, with the armies of heaven following in His train, "clothed in fine linen, white and clean." What a moment of triumph this is! The once-rejected Saviour is returning to earth to establish His kingdom and to reign! Peter confirms that it is "the God of all grace" who has "called us unto his eternal glory by Christ Jesus" (1 Pet.5:10). Grace and glory are combined, the former paving the way for the display of the latter.

What amazing prospects lie before us! We are assured that "if we suffer, we shall also reign with him" (2 Tim.2:12). The sufferings of this present time will pale into insignificance as His glory is revealed and as, by grace, we share that glory with Him.

So Much More!

Paul wrote, "Eye hath not seen, nor ear heard, neither have entered into the heart of man, the things which God hath prepared for them that love him" (1 Cor.2:9). The glories that await us have not been seen by the human eye nor heard in detail by any mortal ear and remain beyond the grasp of our imagination. We could never envisage what it will all be like!

Often *that* verse is quoted, and we stop and go no further. But read on! The verse does not stand alone. It must be understood in its context. Actually Paul is *not* saying that it is all beyond us and that we cannot understand anything. He tells us the very opposite: "But God hath revealed them unto us by his Spirit." The things of heaven and of the life to come are not dark, impenetrable and mysterious. The Holy Spirit of God has made them known to us through the Word! Just as we cannot adequately read another person's thoughts, so we cannot by ourselves fathom the mind of God. A person's own thoughts are only known to that person's spirit; and it is the same with the Triune God. The thoughts of the Almighty are fathomed by the Spirit of God alone — but here is the amazing difference. The Holy Spirit who searches "the deep things of God" has been given to indwell God's children. By His ministry we are enabled to "know the things that are freely given to us of God" (1 Cor.2:10—12).

All too frequently we are impatient and try to hurry things on. We need that word of caution found in 1 Corinthians 4:5: "Therefore judge nothing before the time, until the Lord come, who both will bring to light the hidden things of darkness, and will make manifest the counsels of the hearts: and then shall every man have praise of God." It is *His* evaluation that counts. Our vision is often limited. Many facts presently remain hidden from our view. But when the Lord comes He shall bring that which is hidden into the full light of day. The secret thoughts will then be revealed, and those God deems worthy of receiving praise shall have it from Him.

In the meanwhile we need patience. The "husbandman" who has toiled in the fields sowing and tending the crop must be patient as he awaits the early and latter rains which are both necessary. Indeed, "long patience" is called for as he looks ahead to the seemingly distant harvest. The application is simple. "Be patient therefore, brethren, unto the coming of the Lord." Like the worker in the fields, "be ye also patient ... for the coming of the Lord draweth nigh" (Jas.5:7,8).

Yes, the coming of the Lord *is* drawing nigh! It is His coming that will bring the glories of heaven into the view of those who are waiting for Him. Day by day we need to be "looking for that blessed hope" of His return from heaven (Titus 2:13). It is a "hope" that will motivate us in our service now. There *is* life beyond the sunset: the Lord Jesus Christ is coming back to take His people to that land of everlasting light and life.

The Closing Appeal

As this book reaches its conclusion, some questions need to be raised. Are *you* one of His people? Do you *belong* to the Lord Jesus Christ? Can *you* say that He is your Saviour and that heaven is your home? It is vital that we turn from our sins in true repentance and trust Him as our own personal Saviour. We can only find salvation through His death upon the cross.

The final page of Scripture contains a wonderful invitation. "Let him that is athirst come. And whosoever will, let him take the water of life freely" (Rev.22:17). If you are thirsting for something more, come to the Saviour! Then you will be able to respond to the promise of His return by saying gladly, "Even so, come, Lord Jesus" (Rev.22:20).